MILLION DOLLAR REFERRALS

THE SECRETS TO BUILDING A PERPETUAL CLIENT LIST TO GENERATE A SEVEN-FIGURE INCOME

ALAN WEISS

New York   Chicago   San Francisco   Lisbon
London   Madrid   Mexico City   Milan
New Delhi   San Juan   Seoul
Singapore   Sydney   Toronto

1 2 3 4 5 6 7 8 9 10   DOC/DOC   1 9 8 7 6 5 4 3 2 1

ISBN: 978-0-07-176927-3
MHID: 0-07-176927-7

e-ISBN: 978-0-07-176990-7
e-MHID   0-07-176990-0

Library of Congress Cataloging-in-Publication Data

Weiss, Alan
    Million dollar referrals : the secrets to building a perpetual client list to generate a seven-figure income / by Alan Weiss.
        p. cm.
    ISBN-13: 978-0-07-176927-3 (alk. paper)
    ISBN-10: 0-07-176927-7 (alk. paper)
    1. Business referrals.   2. Customer relations.   3. Business networks.
I. Title.
    HF5438.25.W293   2012
    658.8—dc23   2011023406

This book is printed on acid-free paper.

This book is dedicated to Art Strohmer, whom I met at Merck and has since retired, and who was my first and still my best referral source ever.

CONTENTS

PREFACE

I've always considered referral business to be the "platinum standard" in the acquisition of new clients. (Feel free to use "diamond" or "plutonium" or "iPhone" instead of "platinum" to reflect your own value system!)

I had also always considered referrals to be automatic, and as involuntary as respiration or as suffering when rooting for the home team. But when McGraw-Hill asked me to consider writing this book in our Million Dollar series, it struck me that too few people were successfully obtaining referral business.

Upon closer inspection, my suspicions were borne out: professional services providers (as well as almost anyone in a sales capacity) were not asking for referrals, were asking poorly, or were asking and failing to follow up. Most people I've met who are raging successes in consulting, speaking, training, and related professions—and I'm talking about seven-figure incomes here—claim that they can trace most of today's business *to less than a half-dozen original clients and customers*. I thought that was a ludicrous claim, until I sat down with a calculator, Excel sheets, and an abacus, and arrived at a grand total of four for myself.

And so, I was on to something.

I've assembled the very finest practices in this book, along with a free online, continually updated appendix of sources and performance aids. We'll discuss unlikely sources, unlikely questions, and unlikely results—all from the standpoint of regarding and pursuing referrals as though they were the lifeblood of your business.

Which they are.

If you hear that systolic beat underlying your practice, it's the throbbing of referrals flowing through your professional veins (outgoing) and arteries (incoming). The problem is that many of you are not taking care of your hearts, but instead allowing referral plaque to accumulate.

Fortunately, you've come to the right place for a fitness regimen. You might not like the rigor, but you'll thank me when it's over. Just think of all those endorphins flowing like crazy, and all that business pursuing you madly.

—Alan Weiss
East Greenwich, RI
July 2011

ACKNOWLEDGMENTS

THANKS TO MY EDITORS at McGraw-Hill during this Million Dollar series: Betsy Brown, Mary Glenn, Knox Hudson, Leila Porteous, and Daina Penikas. And thanks to my agent through dozens of books, Jeff Herman.

Special gratitude here to colleagues and Mentor Program members Andrew Sobel and Aviv Shahar for sharing some of their insightful and original views about referral business, and to all those who contributed their "greatest referral."

ABOUT THE AUTHOR

ALAN WEISS is one of those rare people who can say that he is a consultant, speaker, and author and mean it. His consulting firm, Summit Consulting Group, Inc., has attracted clients such as Merck, Hewlett-Packard, GE, Mercedes-Benz, State Street Corporation, Times Mirror Group, the Federal Reserve, the New York Times Corporation, and more than 500 other leading organizations. He has served on the boards of directors of the Trinity Repertory Company, a Tony Award–winning New England regional theater, Festival Ballet, and has chaired the Newport International Film Festival.

His speaking typically includes 30 keynotes a year at major conferences, and he has been a visiting faculty member at Case Western Reserve University, Boston College, Tufts, St. John's, the University of Illinois, the Institute of Management Studies, and the University of Georgia Graduate School of Business. He has held an appointment as adjunct professor in the Graduate School of Business at the University of Rhode Island, where he taught courses on advanced management and consulting skills. He once held the record for selling out the highest-priced workshop (on entrepreneurialism) in the then-21-year history of New York City's Learning Annex. His Ph.D. is in psychology, and he is a member of the American Psychological Society, the American Counseling Association, Division 13 of the American Psychological Association, and the Society for Personality and Social Psychology. He has served on the board of governors of Harvard University's Center for Mental Health and the Media.

Alan is an inductee into the Professional Speaking Hall of Fame and the concurrent recipient of the National Speakers Association Council of Peers Award of Excellence, representing the top 1 percent of professional speakers in the world. He has been named a Fellow of the Institute of Management Consultants (FCMC), one of only two people in history holding both those designations.

His prolific publishing includes more than 500 articles and 44 books, including his bestseller, *Million Dollar Consulting* (from McGraw-Hill). His books have been on the curricula at Villanova, Temple University, and the Wharton School of Business, and have been translated into German, Italian, Arabic, Spanish, Russian, Korean, and Chinese.

He is interviewed and quoted frequently in the media. His career has taken him to 59 countries and 49 states. (He is afraid to go to North Dakota.) *Success* magazine has cited him in an editorial devoted to his work as "a worldwide expert in executive education." The *New York Post* called him "one of the most highly regarded independent consultants in America." He is the winner of the prestigious Axiem Award for Excellence in Audio Presentation.

He is the recipient of the Lifetime Achievement Award of the American Press Institute, the first ever for a nonjournalist, and one of only seven awarded in the 65-year history of the association.

He has coached former and present Miss Rhode Island/Miss America candidates in interviewing skills. He once appeared on the popular American TV game show *Jeopardy*, where he lost badly in the first round to a dancing waiter from Iowa.

CHAPTER 1

BUSINESS RELATIONSHIPS ARE A PROCESS, NOT AN EVENT

HOW TO CREATE LONG-TERM CLIENTS AND CUSTOMERS

THE CHARACTERISTICS OF A RELATIONSHIP BUSINESS

Referrals are recommendations to hire you. This concludes my prepared remark. Questions?

All right, you purchased a 200+-page book, so I'll provide some details. But let's not stray from the basic premise. Every day, people are providing advice, counsel, recommendations, suggestions, and urgings for others to follow in securing personal and professional products and services. If you're like most of us, you've sent people to your attorney, your dentist, your accountant, your auto mechanic, your favorite Internet product site, your favorite vacation property, and so forth. And you've listened to others' similar advice.

> **Listen Up!**
> *For most people, the most credible referrals originate with peers or with recognized and respected experts in a field.*

Business relationships are a process, not an event. That is, they are an ongoing movie, not a static snapshot. The longer you maintain productive and valuable business relationships, the longer you will be the beneficiary of the referrals that can emanate from that source.

Clients have more value than "merely" the fee they pay you! If you view client relationships as long-term and worth maintaining, you can derive

- *Referrals.* The client makes ongoing recommendations to third parties to contact you for projects and engagements.
- *References.* The client serves as a source of credibility and endorsement when you refer prospects to him.
- *Testimonials.* The client provides an "evergreen" endorsement that you can use in print or video on your website and within your marketing materials.
- *Repeat business.* If you are always topical and "on the radar screen," you may have the inside track on future business.
- *Independent credibility.* Recognizable names on your client list add to your credibility and legitimacy.

Those firms that merely "process" clients through their systems are losing longer-term value from those clients and customers. Those that "harangue" clients with constant offers and requests risk driving their goodwill away. Thus, you must reach an intelligent, planned relationship with clients that creates the leverage needed for expanded future business and the reciprocity that the client finds of value in doing so.

In Figure 1.1, you can see that I consider relationships to be as important as products and services. Relationships are based on

- *Trust:* Do you live up to your promises and claims?
- *Value:* Do you demonstrably improve the client's condition?
- *Responsiveness:* Are you accessible, and do you respond rapidly?
- *Credibility:* Does the client feel it's impressive to be partnering with you?
- *Reciprocity:* Do you recommend people to the client where appropriate?
- *Professionalism:* Are you on time and on deadline?
- *Innovation:* Are you leading-edge, state-of-the-art?
- *Reputation:* Are you seen by others as being the best of the best?

The more strong and powerful these factors are, the more you move toward "breakthrough" in Figure 1.1. The more you create and maintain breakthrough relationships, the more you will receive unsolicited referrals from your clients.

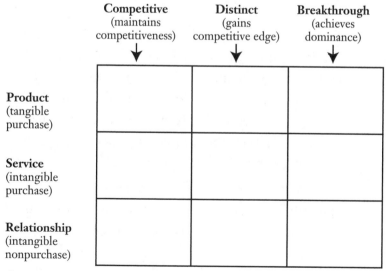

Figure 1.1 Strategic Profile Potential

Of course, there are other sources of referrals, beyond clients. They include friends, professional associates, colleagues, the media, and so forth. However, clients are the most powerful source, since they have actually invested in you, and they are the most credible sources for others who want to invest in you.

A fascinating aspect, however, is that powerful word of mouth creates referrals from people who have never been your clients, but who want to appear to be "in the know" and knowledgeable by having the intelligence to recommend you!

A relationship business is possible with almost any type of organization. It isn't a matter of content, but rather a matter of intent.

Many auto dealers provide a gift or an incentive for a customer who recommends a new customer. We once had a dentist who sent my wife a rose for every person she recommended. I routinely provide a discounted or free seat in one of my workshops for people who bring others to the event. Internet sites often provide coupons and discounts for others.

The nature of a strong relationship business that engenders referrals usually requires

1. *Immediate value.* I'm so impressed that I want others whom I respect to know of your value. Note that this isn't time-dependent, and I don't have to have been using your services for a long time. This is usually promoted through rapid responsiveness, a pragmatic product or service that can be used immediately, and short-term gratification.

2. *Universality.* The wider and more flexible the applicability of your value, the easier it is for me to find people to whom to recommend it. Otherwise, if I have to wait for the "right circumstances," I'll tend to forget about it.

3. *Requests for referrals.* We'll discuss the exact language later, but it's important for you to let me know that you need and seek referrals. A doctor I visited once had a tiny sign in the lobby saying, "We appreciate your referrals." It would have been better if he had mentioned that to his patients, especially those who were delighted with his advice and regimens.

4. *Flexibility and depth.* Ironically, some people who love you won't tend to give you referrals if they suspect that either you won't have time for them or you can't handle any more work. You need to make it clear that you have the resources to handle more business and that your current client will always be a priority for you.

The first step in creating Million Dollar Referrals is to appreciate that they originate in trusting relationships with current and past clients. You must regard those relationships with the same planning and priorities you provide for your products and services.

Referrals are simply another powerful source of current and future revenues.

INITIAL LANGUAGE AND BEHAVIORS TO STIMULATE LEVERAGE

The potential for referral business begins with initial meetings. We'll focus for the moment on business relationships, since clients who partner with you and benefit from the value of your work are your most important referral sources of all.

Here are my suggestions for language to use in four stages of a client relationship:

New Clients, Project Launching

- "As we move forward, it's common for me to request referrals from my client partners, since that is the source of most of my business. I hope you'll consider agreeing to do that when the time is right."

- "Referrals are the 'coinage of my realm' in this business, and I'm going to work very hard to maximize your project's outcomes so that you'll be very comfortable in providing them at the right point."

- "It's very early, but my experience is that it's not uncommon for my clients to want to share their results with others. I want to assure you that when you provide referrals, and if I accept their business, you will always have my highest priority, and I would never endanger that."

- "Since you and I actually met through a referral, you know how effective that can be for others for whom we both believe I may be a good 'fit.' I'm happy to discuss that with you if you are ever questioned about our work together."

- "If you encounter people inside or outside of the organization whom you believe could benefit from my help, I'd be happy to be of further service to you and to them."

Existing Clients, Project Underway

- "As we've progressed, I've received some indirect inquiries from some of your colleagues. Would you be comfortable introducing me?"

- "Would it make sense to approach the other units that have relationships to our project to see if they are amenable to becoming part of it?"

- "When the project began, I mentioned the potential of referrals from you to people who might also benefit from this value. While it may be premature to approach them, it's probably a good time to understand who they may be."

- "Are there people outside of the organization with whom you'd like me to share some of these approaches?"

- "Who else within the organization do you think I should be talking to as this project approaches completion?"

Existing Clients, Project Concluding

- "As I mentioned at the outset and along the way, referrals are the lifeblood of my business. To whom would you be willing to introduce me at this point?"

- "While we're still together, and before this project concludes, as it will soon, can you suggest who else I should be talking to here for similar benefits?"

- "If you had to choose three names of people who might be interested in this type of value, what would they be?"

- "It seems to me there are three logical continuation points for me. Do you agree, and would you introduce me to your counterparts?"

- "You had mentioned several people whom I should meet when the time is right. Are you prepared to introduce me at this point?"

Past Clients, Projects Concluded

- "I thought I'd contact you to provide some things that might be of interest, update you on my work,

and ask if you have anyone whom you would
recommend that I contact."

- "Looking back at our project's results, and forward to
  what's likely in the future, whom in your organization
  would you recommend that I be contacting to
  provide similar value?"

- "Have you met or considered anyone in your
  professional circles outside your organization for
  whom an introduction would be a win/win/win
  dynamic?"

- "I'm making one of my quarterly calls to see how
  you're doing and inquire as to whether you might
  have some people to recommend to me."

- "I've thought of some people with whom it might
  make sense to work, and I was wondering if you had a
  relationship with any of them and might agree to
  introduce me."

Listen Up!
*Some referrals may readily come your way with no
work, but the more discipline and work you put in,
the more referrals you will acquire.*

I know what you're thinking: this is kind of aggressive, or
at least assertive, or certainly stronger than anything you antic-
ipated. Your behaviors will determine your success with referrals. You needn't (and shouldn't) ask all these questions and
make all these statements. I'm simply giving you options and
showing you that there's a range of approaches you can use at
various junctures in the existing client relationship.

Your behavior must reflect your language and vice versa
(that is, walk the talk and talk the walk). Your clear intent must
be to bring *value* to colleagues of your buyer, hence, the

repeated use of this term in the language just given. It's not about getting business; it's about sharing the value.

Consequently, your behavior and use of such language will be dealing with these variables:

- Preparing the buyer very early—from prior to the project launch—for the idea that you are expecting referrals as a normal part of your relationship. This "sets the stage" for more assertive language to come later, but it also removes the possibility of the buyer saying later, "I had no idea," or "Why didn't you tell me earlier?"
- Assuring the buyer that his own best interests will not suffer from
  - Your time being shared with others[1]
  - Your expertise being used by an internal "rival"
  - Your focus on the buyer diminishing
  - The current project being hastily completed
- Trying to maximize the worth of the referral:
  - A peer or better of your buyer (for example, another buyer).
  - A personal introduction over "just use my name" is not as good.
  - "Please keep my name out of it" is certainly not as good.
- Maximizing the number of referrals from any one source, over time.

[1] Unbelievably, many consultants fail to get referral business because their buyers incorrectly believe that the consultant cannot handle "too much" business at once. A good reply for that is, "Does your company ever turn down business because it has too much, and/or fail to deliver because you have too much business?"

These are the basics of the language, attitude, and behavior you should try to create and manifest in order to maximize your referral success. You can adapt them to your style and culture, but you must be relatively assertive in pursuing them. The last thing you want to hear, which too many of us have heard, is: "So many people ask about you and there are still others I'd love to recommend you to, but I realize you're just too busy and too selective to need this kind of volume."

THE CRITERIA FOR HIGH-POTENTIAL, LONG-TERM CLIENTS

Long-term clients create long-term referrals, an endless and renewable source of future business. This is like finding a gold mine, only easier; like hitting a hot stock when it was a $6 per-share start-up, only easier; like hitting the trifecta at the track, only easier; and like getting the best table at every restaurant, only much easier.

So if it's so easy, why isn't it being done every day?

One key issue is that we don't recognize the criteria for high-potential clients. I pointed out earlier that many of the most successful people can point to a mere handful of important sources for *all* of their current business. Those sources may already exist for you, or they could be just around the block or underfoot, but if you don't know how to recognize them, they're no more important than any other client or prospect.

I've also found that many successful professional services providers never change their original mentality of "business at any price or cost." That means that while once, when they were hungry, they intelligently sought and captured every available piece of business that was on their radar screen (I remember doing $25 career counseling sessions), they still have that same nagging fear of never eating again, even though the refrigerator is currently fully stocked (and isn't their only larder).

We need to lose the desperation mentality and adapt an abundance mentality, to stop fearing losing and start rejoicing in winning.

Therefore, we don't need every single potential piece of business, we are not being rejected, and we are not personally without worth if someone chooses not to do business with us, and there is some business (quite a lot of business) that we choose not to accept.

> **Listen Up!**
> *Every year you should be abandoning about 15 percent of your least profitable, least interesting, lowest potential, and most troublesome business. Not only don't you need this business, but you can't reach out to new business unless you let go of old business.*

Who are your ideal clients? That is, which of the clients that you are currently working with or have previously worked with have the most value? And which prospects are the most attractive to you?

Here are some criteria, which you should modify according to your business, your temperament, and your strategy:

- *Revenues.* The likelihood of their providing significant (six-figure) income over a period of years from a variety of buyers.
- *Profit.* The ability to meet the client's objectives with a minimum of overhead, such as personal visits, subcontracted staff, special technology, and so on.

- *Referral potential.* The client's ability and willingness to create relationships with other buyers internally and externally.
- *Reference potential.* The degree to which the client will gladly serve as a reference point in writing, on video, or electronically for other prospects you develop.
- *Prestige.* The cachet and automatic credibility you garner from citing this organization as a client, and its immediate recognition by others.
- *Interest.* The degree to which the work is exciting, a "stretch," and a potential laboratory for you to try new methodologies and new approaches.

Add to these or modify them as you wish, but this set of criteria should help you determine

1. Which of your current clients you should do the most to retain and develop, and seek referrals from.
2. Which prospects you should direct your marketing toward and try the most to retain visibility with.

What you emerge with is your personal gold mine, stock, pari-mutuel bet, and table on the water. You've arranged it, without the need for luck, survey equipment, financial theories, tips to the captain, or touts.

I relate Hal's story to you because your high-potential clients and referral sources can be deceiving. I was young and without much money. But I could afford basic insurance (in fact, I had to have it), I was on my way up, and I had a lot of other young friends who were starting families and were on their way up.

CASE STUDY: The Irrepressible Insurance Impresario

When I was 22 years of age and newly married, I went to work at Prudential Insurance in home office management. My wife was a teacher, and between us we had zero money after paying the rent.

One day, Hal Mapes, an agent from Prudential, arrived at our apartment door and informed me that his main prospects included new members of management. He convinced me of the logic of buying Prudential insurance ("Think about your career").[2] He then asked me for "three names."

When I told him I didn't know whom to recommend, he prompted me about college friends, work colleagues, community acquaintances, family mem- bers, and so on. Every six months he would return like clockwork, first to see if we needed more insurance, and second to get his three names. (Once, when I told him I would not give him three names, he simply asked my wife for another cup of coffee and didn't budge. I gave him three names.)

Hal probably had 200 clients, which meant 400 visits, which resulted in 1,200 names. If he closed just 10 percent, that was 120 new policies, each with about a $2,000 commission over time. And the next year, of course, he had 320 clients, 640 visits, 1,920 names—you get the idea.

He retired a wealthy man merely by asking for three names.

[2] I bought the cheapest policy possible, which I believe didn't even include burial. Apparently, you were thrown off a moving train outside of Secaucus, New Jersey.

Metaphorically, are you establishing relationships with (and attracting) clients whom you can ask for "three names"? That's really what we're talking about here, and I don't want to make this any more complicated than that. Direct income from clients is wonderful, but it is only one of the sources of client value. The (1) ability and (2) willingness to provide referral business is a close second.

I worked with Merck, the pharmaceutical giant, for more than a dozen years. During five of them, Merck was named

"America's Most Admired Company" by the annual *Fortune* magazine poll of executives. Over the course of 30 projects, I was paid about $2.5 million. But during that time—and particularly over those five years—I attracted twice that much business from Merck's referrals and from Merck's serving as a high-profile reference. If I were good enough for the best, I was good enough for the next prospect.

I often talk about "thinking of the fourth sale first." You also have to think about the ROF: return on referrals.

THE 10 CRITICAL DOS AND DON'TS

The 10 things it is essential to accomplish for powerful, high-potential business relationships are

1. Deal exclusively with the true economic buyer (the person who can sign a check) at the outset, and deal regularly with that buyer throughout the project. Don't allow yourself to be delegated downward or to lose touch. Insist on the reciprocity of rapid responses for both of you, and acquire private e-mail, phone, and cell phone addresses.

2. Be diagnostic in your marketing efforts, but be prescriptive in your delivery and methodology. During your acquisition stage, it's fine to ask where the prospect is, where the prospect stands, and what the prospect desires. But once you have the business relationship and the project, the client wants guidance and your best advice, not, "Well, what do you think?" Save that for the therapist's couch.

3. Provide extra value along the way. Don't expand the project by taking on more work than you're

contracted to do, but do suggest ideas and improvements based on your professional observation. The client may choose to implement them independently or may ask you for another proposal. But the point is to be a source of continuing input for organizational improvement.

4. **Move fast.** The more quickly the client sees improvement, the better off and happier she will be. Find rapid, "easy" initial victories to create positive momentum and a perception of success early on.

5. **Transfer skills to the client to perpetuate the gains.** Don't be proprietary about your intellectual property and methodologies. Equip the client to self-direct and implement under your guidance. This will solidify the impact and prevent the collapse that can happen if you're the only one holding things together.

6. **Raise the bar.** Mere problem solving is not that valuable (it merely restores past performance) and is readily accomplished by the client in any case, given the myriad of skills and techniques available today. See that you create improvement *over and above* the client's current and satisfactory condition. New levels of performance are where the most dramatic ROI resides.

7. **Share credit.** Readily provide kudos to client personnel for helping, assisting, improving, and generally ensuring the success of the project. This enables you to be seen as "one of the team" and not "the outsider."

8. **Create new relationships throughout the project duration.** Reach out to other buyers, invite other

areas to view the results, and share information with others. So long as your buyer approves, find ways to create multidimensional and varied relationships throughout the organization.

9. Make success visible. Use client media (intranet, newsletters, magazines, and so forth) to explain and promote the project's success and impact. Create great publicity for the project, with you as a part of the team.

10. Use the client as a reference base and part of your client list. If others ask your client about you, ironically, it keeps your name and past successes in front of your client and frequently in mind.

Listen Up!
Your project may be a 50/50 proposition between you and your buyer, but your ability to create a long-term, powerful relationship is 85 percent your initiative.

Here are the things to avoid on your way to a long-term client relationship. I could have said, "The reverse of the 10 above," but I want to be specific about some additional land mines:

1. Don't engage in endless information gathering and consensus building. Get on with the project. Don't fall victim to the often-true bromide: "A consultant is someone who arrives to study a problem, and stays on to become part of it."

2. Don't become overly friendly and collaborative with the HR and training people. You do *not* want to be seen as a peer of these folks, but rather as a peer of the buyer. They may love you, and they may be

heavily engaged in the implementation, but don't let them become your regular chums. HR is, deservedly, one of the least credible (and least powerful) elements of any organization.

3. **Don't lavish insufficient attention on the client.** Clients (and buyers) want to believe that they are your highest priority and that they are special. Find ways to make them feel it, and do so often. But this leads to point 4.

4. **Don't spend inordinate amounts of time with the client, or fall victim to inappropriate labor intensity.** Clients can feel good, "in the loop," and well taken care of *without your physical presence*. Find ways to use technology, the client's own resources, and judicious personal visits to create a great relationship without living there (and thereby jeopardizing other potential great relationships).

5. **Don't disengage without next steps.** That may involve quarterly follow-ups, agreement to send your monthly newsletter to 100 people, a semiannual audit, or whatever. Never walk away "for good." Always plan something else, whether or not it involves revenue.

6. **Don't try to create a flying goat by strapping wings on it and throwing it out of an airplane.** By that I mean, be honest—don't cover up your shortcomings or failures. Treat your buyer as a true partner who deserves to know what's going wrong and why, and what he has to do about it using appropriate internal clout.

7. **Don't take advantage.** For example, submit reasonable amounts for expense reimbursement,

but don't charge for lavish meals, alcohol, postage, suites, or "administrative support." No matter how large the client, you will eventually be found out. Don't "borrow" equipment or materials from the client. Treat the client as a trusted friend, not an ATM machine. (I don't even charge clients for mileage.)

8. Don't be an ideologue about methodology. You may have a "six-step sales sequence to success," but the client may need only four steps, may also need a seventh, or may hate your fifth. Go with the flow. Change what you must instead of insisting on arbitrary delivery options. Use the client's culture as your guide, not your own.

9. Don't be paranoid. Allow the client to have copies of slides and templates; encourage recording of small meetings; share your own intellectual property. Assume the client is as honest as you are. (If that means that you are suspicious of the client, figure out what that says about you!) Don't treat the client's personnel as if they're thieves in the night.

10. Don't be tone-deaf. Listen for opportunities. Avoid being consumed by your current project to such an extent that you miss the potential for providing additional value and developing longer-term relationships. Don't operate in an isolation ward.

At any given time, these guidelines will help you view any given client as the long-term resource you should be continually seeking. That's why I call it a "process" and not an "event."

You want to create an ongoing source of business and, sometimes even more important, business referrals. (There may be only so much work to be done with a single client, but the potential for referrals is virtually limitless.)

THE BEST POSITIONING FOR YOU

Your positioning within a client (not as a brand or generically) should depend on these factors:

1. The nature of your project and its impact
2. Your relationship with the buyer or buyers
3. The recognition factor of the client
4. Your ability to cite the client and your work
5. Your chutzpah[3]

1. The Nature of Your Project and Its Impact

Your positioning will be dependent on the type of project you are doing and the difference its outcome represents for your client. We've discussed earlier, for example, the higher value and visibility of innovation (raising the standard of performance) as compared to problem solving (restoring the old level of performance).

---

[3] This is a technical consulting term, generally referring to one's "courageous nature."

CASE STUDY: Merck and Diversity

I was asked if I would help in the baseline (first) study of diversity at Merck. Since the study methodology we agreed upon comprised focus groups, interviews, observation, and surveys, it was ideal for me. What was needed was not a diversity "expert," but rather an expert on evaluating behavior and beliefs.

As a result of my work and that of others, Merck embarked on a much more aggressive campaign to foster diversity in ethnicity, culture, race, religion, beliefs, origins, and so on, under the guidance of then-CEO Roy Vagelos. This included what we called "heroic" efforts to find, recruit, and nurture a variety of people.

This was high-impact and very public, talked about throughout the organization. I chose (wisely) not to position myself before or after the engagement as a diversity expert, but rather as an organizational development consultant who focused on the processes of improvement, not the content.

2. Your Relationship with the Buyer or Buyers

The "tighter" (more trusting) your relationship with your buyers, the more you can position yourself in certain perspectives, such as a "strategist" because you work with CEOs or a "sales accelerator" because you work with vice presidents of sales.

3. The Recognition Factor of the Client

Not all clients, no matter how much they love you, are valuable positioning sources because no one else knows of them. They may be specialized within an industry, relatively small, better known in other countries, or deliberately maintaining a low profile.

CASE STUDY: Hewlett-Packard and Change

HP was a client with tremendous talent and confidence. It routinely worked on projects with top internal people and a half-dozen external consultants from different firms, concurrently. HP believed that this combination created the best thinking and destructive testing of new ideas. "We don't want to get stuck breathing our own exhaust," my buyer was fond of saying.

During one marathon session, everyone had talked and explored and talked some more. I had kept quiet, trying to understand the impasse. Finally, I walked up to the whiteboard without invitation and drew a visual describing why we were stuck and how to break the logjam. Everyone agreed (perhaps because they were eager to get home), and the meeting adjourned on a positive note.

The next day, my buyer handed me a plum assignment. "You are obviously the top change management expert around here," she said, "so we won't be needing a roomful of people anymore."

From that time on, I was able to position myself as a change management expert with my buyer's complete and generous endorsement.

CASE STUDY: The Federal Reserve and Shredded Money

It was quite an ordeal to pass muster with the Federal Reserve Bank of New York; it included three formal meetings in front of different people and a legal review that changed my 2.5-page proposal into 32 pages (I am *not* making this up) without, unbelievably, changing anything substantive.

I decided early on not only that the business was wonderful and worth fighting for, but also that having the "Fed" on my client list would be invaluable, because its customers were major financial institutions that were my customers and prospects.

The toughest part was that, periodically, a new acquaintance at the Fed would ask if I'd like a million dollars, then, after a proper delay, produce a package of shredded money equaling a million. The first time it was funny.

Thus, it's best to find the "high flyers" to add to your client list and nurture them to improve your positioning and your ability to create other long-term clients.

4. Your Ability to Cite the Client and Your Work

Some firms may be unknown, but some highly known firms don't want to be known—at least, not on your client list. Thus, a major aspect of positioning is to find and use the names of recognizable clients who don't mind being cited.

This is often easy, so long as you don't discuss the nature of any confidential or sensitive work. But it's often tricky, especially if anyone, at any time, contacts the legal department.

CASE STUDY: The First Breath

I organized my conversation and a great deal of my collateral material and introductions so that a "critical mass of critical names" emerged immediately. In other words, once I say, "I've worked with JPMorgan Chase, Mercedes, Toyota, HP, the Federal Reserve, GE, and IBM," the other party is generally nodding and asking me the next question or inviting me to sit down before I can take another breath and continue the list.

I use these names very strategically and for highest impact. Companies' reputations rise and fall. Arthur Andersen used to be one of my "first breath" names, but it had to be removed. Your positioning will be quickly enhanced by your ability to develop and nurture enough marquee names to fill that first breath.

5. Your Chutzpah

There is no case study needed here. Your willingness to "blow your own horn" and let people know of your successes, track record, and "war stories" is vital to your positioning.

Perception is reality. People act based on what they perceive. They often perceive a solo practitioner in any professional services work as being "between jobs," acting as a subcontractor, or appropriate only for small businesses. It's up to you to change that perception by creating the perception—the positioning—that you think best.

The first step in Million Dollar Referrals is creating high-quality, long-term client relationships that serve as the basis for those referrals. The next step is to ensure that these remain as annuities.

THE ANNUITY FACTOR

I WILL STILL LOVE YOU IN THE MORNING

CREATING A MILLION DOLLAR CONSULTING® ACCELERANT CURVE

The Million Dollar Consulting© Accelerant Curve is designed to give you some guidance on how to attract the type of clients and perpetual referrals that are best for you.

The vertical axis in Figure 2.1 is decreasing barriers to entry—that is, making it easy to know you and your work and results. The horizontal axis is increasing fees, which result from higher value and increased intimacy with you and your work.

Solely considering those two axes, you can see that the easier it is for people to appreciate your work, the more people will seek more of a relationship and more intimacy with you, moving, for example, from free downloads on your site, to the purchase of products, to participation in a teleconference, to registration for a workshop, to personal coaching, to consulting work, to retainer, and so on.

As a client "slides" down the Accelerant Curve, trust and branding grow commensurately. Along the way, "bounce fac-

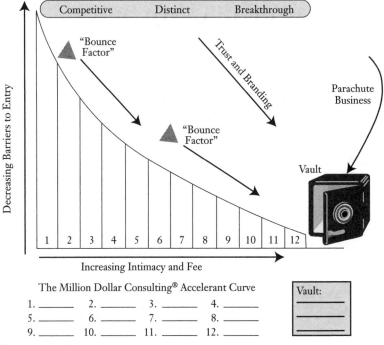

Figure 2.1   The Accelerant Curve

tors" can speed things along (for example, someone reads one of my books and decides to make a "leap" into my Mentor Program). The verticals you see representing your offerings (no matter what type of business you're in) tend to be competitive on the left (most people offer something similar), distinct in the middle (there are distinguishing features about you), and breakthrough toward the right (only you provide such products and services).

Eventually, you have what I call a "vault" that houses your unique offerings, which may include retainers, licensing, electronic applications, and so forth. As your brand and your reputation increase, "parachute business" is drawn directly to these high-end, high-value, high-fee offerings without the necessity to proceed down the Accelerant Curve. At these points, one's entire Accelerant Curve may shift to the right, with a higher fee required for entry even on the left, because of your reputation.

There is no magic number of verticals, but take a few minutes now or when you finish this segment or chapter to define how many offerings you have and how they are distributed. Too many people are focused solely on the left, the middle, or the right. That means there are "chasms" and clients can't easily increase their work with you gradually over time. You must have a diversity of offerings in place, spread along the curve, and manifest so that your prospects and clients can readily identify them with you.

That means that you speak about them, publicize them, write about them, mention them in conversation, gain testimonials about them, and so on.

Listen Up!
You can't be a one-trick pony, or the only referrals you'll receive will be for that one trick.

If you find you have gaps, determine how you'll fill them in.

Ironically, as you move from left to right, labor intensity usually *declines*. That seems like a paradox, since value and intimacy increase. But you'll find that people are quite happy with relatively brief moments if they know they have access; electronic and "remote" abilities can create very rapid responsiveness; and merely the fact that someone knows you're there (for example, on retainer) carries great comfort.

The lessons for referral business include these:

- As clients progress down the curve, they are capable of providing referrals for everything that has preceded the place where they are. Never be content with a single referral for a single offering, or merely with "character references." It's far better to have someone say, "If you're looking for the best strategy implementation expert I know . . . "

- Make sure you "seed" your events and promotions with existing clients who are far down the slope. For example, if you host a breakfast for 15 prospects, make sure you have at least 3 clients among the group. They will sing the praises of *all* that they have been through far more credibly than you can. (One of my favorite clients is someone who walks through a room of peers saying, "You *must* engage in this experience with Alan. It's changed my business. You can't wait. Do it today!"

- Accelerate "vault" business by focusing on referrals from your very best customers and clients. Don't spend too much time with referrals from the left, "competitive" side; focus on those who took the leap and engaged you in high-value work right from the outset, and who can encourage others to do so. The Accelerant Curve works nicely on its own, but your prompting should always be for "breakthrough" relationships.

- Choose a point on the curve—say, a third of the way or halfway over—when you ensure that you're following the earlier advice to begin the serious request for referral business. Let that be your "trigger" point.

I hope you're beginning to appreciate that a client's value to you is more than merely the total of the cashed checks and credit card receipts. And the strategies and tactics for building long-term referral value can be an intrinsic part of your client interaction. You can methodically include referral building almost from the initial point of contact, but certainly from des-ignated points that you create along the way. The more valu-able the client, the more this is vital.

Whether you choose to use the Accelerant Curve or not (although I can't imagine why on earth you wouldn't), you'll need some metrics to help you judge when to maximize your ability to garner and utilize referrals from the most valuable sources. The "physics" of fees are simple: it's far better to have one $100,000 client than ten $10,000 clients—profit margins are higher, and labor intensity is far lower.

Once you're adept at this, the question now becomes how best to create that referral from the individual who can best pro-vide it. Companies don't give referrals, people do.

The onus is on you to decide how you'll deal with each buyer and significant potential referral source.

ADJUSTING TO THE STYLES OF BUYERS

Buyers, who are also our chief referral source, have a wide vari-ety of styles, as do we all. I haven't experienced an "ideal" lead-ership style, for example. My experience points more toward leaders being successful by being flexible in dealing with oth-ers, but also being consistent about how they handle key issues. (In other words, acting the same about ethics or urgency or opportunity, and not being situational and unpredictable.)

I've seen buyers who are aggressive, friendly, authorita-tive, consensus building, analytic, and highly risk taking. They can all be successful or unsuccessful, *and they can all be strong referral sources or weak referral sources.*

It's incumbent upon us to adapt to the style of the buyer (or any other referral source that you want to include—I'm simply focusing on the most obvious, frequent, and important one here). We've already discussed timing and preparation in terms of alerting the buyer that you'll be asking and providing guidelines for timing. Assuming that you've done all that well, here are some techniques based on varying types of referral sources.

1. The Validator

This is a person who is happy, but who wants to "wait to see what the final results look like." The problem is that "the final results" in this person's mind can be years away! The resolution here is to focus on the objectives and metrics of your project, and point out that certain interventions have certainly proven their worth.

Example response: "Would you agree to provide some referrals based on the fact that the first six people coached have already shown higher average new business sales after just 90 days? We know that to be true, and I'm sure you know some people who would be delighted with that result for their own operations."

2. The Skeptic

Ironically, the greater the short-term success, the more some people are prone to question whether you were really the key cause of the improvement! When you exceed expectations dramatically, you can find yourself in the unlikely position of being "too good." You need to demonstrate your exact contributions and the etiology of the intervention and the result.

Example response: "I worked with the members of your top team for 30 days, after which they are holding only half as many meetings, and you have indicated that the requests for you to 'referee' amongst them have disappeared. Obviously, if we hadn't changed things, the old behaviors would have simply persevered."

3. The Disclaimer

Some buyers will tell you that what you've done is so unique that they really can't think of anyone else who can use your help. They will "give it some thought," but they're really at a loss as to whom to recommend. (This may be real or an equivocation, but it doesn't matter.)

Example response: "Let me offer some suggestions. You're running a subsidiary, as are four of your colleagues. Although the content is different, the process of strategy implementation we've used can be applied to each. Why don't we start with those four? Would you introduce me?"

4. The Collector

This buyer doesn't want to share you. In the previous chapter, we discussed the real fear of losing your priority attention because of the volume of business you have, and the irrational fear of helping internal competitors.

Example response: "I'll guarantee you the exact same level of attention and responsiveness you have with me now, but surely you can respect my own need to grow my business so that I can develop more resources to help you still more? Can you cite me an instance in which your own operation turned down business because you might have too much?!"

5. The Delayer

For many people, any issue that isn't directly affecting them is, by definition, low priority. People will procrastinate by saying,

"Just give me a little more time." They're often quite sincere, but they're also quite frustrating in that the "little bit of time" becomes an eternity.

Example response: "I know how busy you are, and I also know that you do have some very good prospective referrals for me. Let's just talk through them right now, while we're already together (or on the phone; never by e-mail). Can we take just three minutes to name four or five people? For example, what about . . . ?"

6. The Superficialist

To your immediate gratification, you receive a dozen referrals when you ask. But as you begin to pursue them, you find that they are at the wrong level, are not really known to the originator, have no relevant need, and so on. You have quantity but not quality.

Example response: "After I spoke to a couple of the people on your list, I realized that I've made a small mistake in not explaining carefully what makes sense for all of us. The people I need to talk to are people like you: at your level, in need of this kind of value, and personally known by you. Can you help me sort out the rest of this list or add people to it?"

7. The Jurist

You'll sometimes hear, despite earlier inquiries from you about potential, "I've double-checked with our legal department, and it turns out that I really can't give you referrals because of competitive situations, liability, and so on. I never realized it would be this difficult."

Example response: "We have several options here. For example, you can give me personal referrals, such as people from your club or your social network, not at all connected with the company. Or you can simply give me some names without an introduction and allow me to say that I know you and have worked with you, without disclosing any content. Or you can give me names with the provision that I won't use your name at all. Which of these can work?"

8. The Unreachable

On occasion, you'll find that calls and e-mail on this subject are not returned, even though you speak with the buyer about other things, and despite the fact that the buyer has previously said that referrals are fine at some point. You need to be more aggressive here.

Example response: "Alan, while we're talking about the great results of the restructuring, I thought of three people I want to run by you as potential clients for me. You know them all, and I'd like to use your name and perhaps even obtain a personal introduction." (This is bold, but you have nothing to lose at this point.)

Prepare yourself for these contingencies. And don't forget, these are exceptions. If you've prepared the proper groundwork, most referral sources will proactively say, "I have another couple of people you really ought to meet. When can you call them?"

WHY AND WHEN PERCEPTIONS OF VALUE *FOLLOW* HIGHER FEES

The mantra in professional services is that the higher your value, the more you can charge. (If you're charging by the hour or the day, or in six-minute increments as attorneys do, stop reading immediately and pick up *Million Dollar Consulting* or *Value-Based Fees*. Otherwise, you're not going to appreciate what follows.)

If you see a progression from competitive, to distinct, to breakthrough in your offerings, you can understand how the last is worth more than the first two. Thus, coaching a midlevel manager is something that gazillions of people can do, but forming internal accountability groups to perpetuate growth every day is much more distinctive, and providing unlimited access to you by e-mail and phone for external support is breakthrough. (This applies to everything from buying a car, where the salesperson uses a "configurator" to allow you to design the car on the computer and see the results, to pizza delivery, where some operations guarantee delivery in 40 minutes or it's free. There is always a way to distinguish yourself, your products, your services, and your relationships.)

The fascinating aspect, however, is that "breakthrough" perceptions are often created by *the very act of raising fees significantly above those of the competition.*

Think of Brioni, Bulgari, and Bentley, three of my favorite "Bs." You don't need them in order to dress well, tell the time, or have effective transportation. But because of their perceived excellence, cachet, and ego satisfaction, they can charge whatever they like. (Before the entire automobile world changed, GM would tell its designers that they had to create a Buick that would sell for $18,000 and provide the company with a margin of 20 percent. Mercedes would tell its designers to build the safest, best-performing car they could; once it had the car, it would then decide what to charge for it.)

Figure 2.2 shows a relationship I'd like you to consider.

In the graphic, as time goes on and your reputation and brand improve, the lines cross. You're now perceived as being so strong and influential in your field that the very fact that you

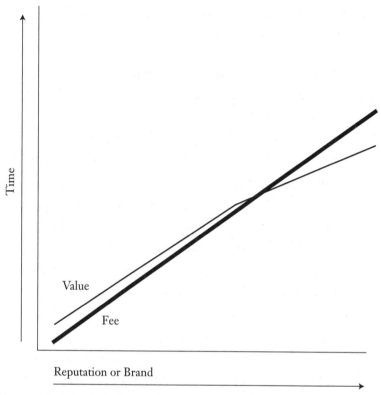

Figure 2.2 When Value Follows Fee

can charge as much as you do indicates your quality. It does seem paradoxical, but think of your own purchases. Many senior people love to brag that they have the best coach money can buy (along with their Baume & Mercier and their Mercedes).

The lines cross when your brand becomes so strong that it attracts people to you, making fee of little concern. That is also the point with the strongest gravity for referral business. Your clients actually love to give your name to others because this magnanimous act shines favorably on them, as well. After all, they found you, have utilized your help, and have been able to afford you.

What takes you to that point? Where do your lines cross? Here are some suggestions:

- You are providing thought leadership in your profession and/or niche. People see you as one of the highest authorities in your specialty.
- You pump intellectual property into the environment. You are a source of new ideas and techniques that are pragmatic and applicable for your clients and prospects. You turn intellectual capital (theory) into tangible application (intellectual property). This process is known as *instantiation*.
- You are an object of interest to others. You do things and attract people that are exciting and newsworthy.
- You use clever phrases and metaphors. I often cite my TIAABB (there is always a bigger boat) to demonstrate why people shouldn't merely always try to obtain the "biggest" or the "most." Your models and methodology are memorable.
- There are significant peripheral benefits from using your services. There may be private newsletters, dedicated websites, global chat rooms, "hot lines," and the opportunity to meet peers who themselves are of great interest. Your clients actually improve *their* brands by citing their relationship with you.

Referrals flow best downhill. That is, the greater the gravitational pull, and the fewer the bumps, logs, boulders, and obstacles in the way, the faster and surer the referrals. When you create very strong brands, you create that steep slope.

What you should be becoming familiar with in these opening chapters is that Million Dollar Referrals are not "average" or "usual" referrals. They rely on special kinds of clients

> **Listen Up!**
> *The ultimate brand is your name. You can have a multiplicity of brands, but you can't beat someone saying, "Get me Anna Smith" in the same way people once said, "Get me IBM" or "Get me McKinsey."*

(or others) and special kinds of relationships, fostered by your reputation and your accomplishments.

Just as you'd want to pursue clients who represent high potential fees and ongoing business, and who have a tradition of using external help, you would also seek those individuals within clients who can provide the most dramatic, effective, and long-lived referrals. The more well known you are, the more you can charge, the more you can legitimately promote your successes, and the more you can expect to gain dramatic referrals from clients.

Here's one of the underlying secrets: when people pay a lot, their expectations are high, *and their own propensity to fulfill those expectations is high*. That's right, someone relatively unknown would have a tougher time influencing a tough, high-level audience. But someone with the reputation for thrilling these audiences and challenging them will find it easier to thrill and challenge them!

In other words, when you're rolling downhill, you keep picking up momentum.

THE CLIENT POTENTIAL BELL CURVE

It's one thing to talk about finding and retaining high-value clients, but *how* does one do that with efficiency and effectiveness on a continual basis? At first blush, *any* client who is interested is a good client! When you have to put bread on the table, such interest becomes extraordinary.

Yet professional services providers spend far too much time on low- and medium-level prospects, allowing themselves less time to acquire the true high-priority prospects. When I was a kid, there was an apparatus in the playground called "monkey bars." The objective was to hold on to the overhead bars and traverse them to the other side, using only your hands, with your feet dangling. (I've learned over the years that these things existed all over the world; such is the culture of play.)

I would grab the first overhead bar, peer down at what looked to me like a thousand-foot drop, and cling for dear life. Inevitably my arms cramped, and I fell the two feet to the ground. Some of my friends, however, raced across, *counterintuitively letting go with one hand to reach out to the next bar*. That's the first time it struck me that you had to let go in order to reach out.

The identical phenomenon applies to all of us today. You can't reach out (to new, high-priority clients and referral sources) if you refuse to let go (of current, low-priority clients and the pursuit of more of the same). As I watched consultants—even very fine marketers—continue to indiscriminately pursue eclectic prospects, I wondered how to rationalize the process.

I compared what I was doing to two other highly successful thought leaders: Seth Godin (*Purple Cow*, amongst other books) and Marshall Goldsmith (*Mojo*, amongst other books), and I discerned what people with strong brands have tended to do.

We are operating at an extreme of the normal distribution of clients because we see that distribution (intentionally or unintentionally) in a third dimension. Take a look at Figure 2.3.

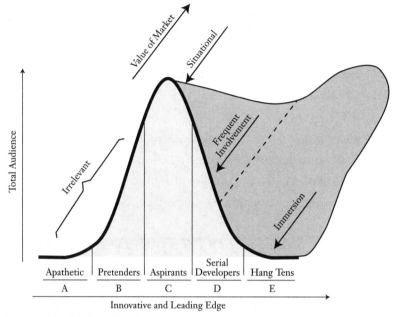

Figure 2.3 Market Value Bell Curve

The left axis is the total constituency you can expect for your products and services, without restriction. Too many people will tell you that their audience is "everyone," but that's simply never true. However, many professional services providers can have quite large potential audiences if there are no restraints, as we'll see in a moment.

The horizontal axis is how innovative and leading-edge the potential audience is. Thus, in this distribution, as we move from left to right, the categories are

- *Apathetic.* These people may nominally be prospects, but they do not care about such offerings from anyone. They may be unprepared or simply arrogant, but the result is the same.

- *Pretenders.* People in this audience segment act as if they are serious; they may attend association meetings and pay lip service to development, but they are seldom purchasers of substantial help.

The first two segments are irrelevant in terms of soliciting high-value clients and referral sources.

- *Aspirants.* These are more serious prospects in terms of considering your offerings, but they are very situational. Your appeal to them may depend on timing, circumstances, or peer pressure.

The third dimension of the bell curve begins to be meaningful from this point on.

- *Serial developers.* These are people who are serious about their own development and that of their people. They will regularly engage in hiring external help, although they tend to budget for it, compare offerings, and plan carefully.
- *Hang tens.* From the old surfing lingo, these are prospects who take prudent risks, want to ride the toughest waves from the front, and are very early experimenters. They will seek out people with novel and/or widely discussed innovative methodologies (hence, the appeal of strong brands and intellectual property). These people can be totally immersed, with their organizations, in your approaches.

Listen Up!
Not all prospects are equal. You must consider the quality of your constituency, not merely the volume.

I've labeled these A to E because of the old ticket system at Disneyland, where the "E ticket" was the one that gained you access to the best rides.[1]

My advice to all professional services providers—particularly those with established firms and practices, strong brands, and evolving intellectual property—is to consciously and deliberately focus on penetrating the extreme right-hand side of my bell curve. The *value of the market* you serve is reflected in that third dimension, but we're too often lulled into pursuing leads in the middle and on the left *because they are easier—people who merely inquire, can't buy, are trying to show they are players, and so forth*.

The annuity factor in referrals is complementary to the annuity factor with great clients. Those that are smart, successful (they have money), and eager to lead the pack are the best bets for both. The hang tens I've described are those who are very eager to invest in products and services that will enable them, personally, to excel and their organizations, as a whole, to create market dominance.

Capturing 20 percent of the D market and 10 percent of the E market is hugely more important than acquiring 50 percent of your personal A to C markets. The revenue per client will be higher, the repeat business rate will be higher, the rate of referrals will be far higher, and the quality of those referrals will be significantly higher. Just as a single $100,000 project is more profitable and less labor-intensive than ten $10,000 projects, so too will the value of the referrals be that much higher in those circumstances.

[1] When asked what it's like to be married to me, my wife used to say I was a "D ticket," mistaking this for the highest degree. Her friends would nod in sympathy. At least, I think it was a mistake.

ALLOWING THE BUYER TO BUY (MORE AND MORE)

Before we leave this topic of "annuity clients," I'd like to reinforce the fact that buyers buy. That's why we call them "buyers."

The idea is to not get in the way.

That sounds ridiculously obvious, but my experience highlights the exact opposite: too many service providers louse up their own sales, their own credibility, and their own value by impeding the buyer's ability to buy.

Here are the key factors.

1. Never "Pitch"

You're a peer of the buyer. Peers don't blatantly sell to one another. They recommend and suggest courses of action that can legitimately assist their peers. (Trust is the fervent belief that the other person has your sincere best interests in mind.)

The stereotypical "elevator pitch" is one of the stupidest pieces of advice in all of salesdom (similar to the "imagine the audience naked" among professional speakers). It's so colossally stupid that I scarcely know where to begin with it. But I do know that I don't like to hear a sales pitch that I didn't solicit, particularly on private time. I'd stop the elevator, throw the barker off, and resume my vertical trip.

No matter where you are—in an office or a conveyance of any kind—don't become a trained seal. People might laugh at you, but they won't jump in and hunt squid with you.

2. Eschew the PowerPoint®

Whenever I see a PowerPoint (or similar technology) presentation, I think of timeshare salespeople or intrusive Web pop-

I walked into a meeting of four partners in a start-up that was seeking a consultant. They each had a favorite, and we were called in separately to chat. I walked in with only my Filofax® diary and placed it on the table.

I saw the vice president of sales hand the CEO (my contact) ten dollars. I learned later that the CEO had bet the other three that I'd be the only one not making a formal presentation and would, in fact, have minimal material of any kind.

They gave me the job.

ups. Technology has a way of superseding the personal relationship (which is why this is deadly in speaking, because the attention is on the technology, not the speaker).

The more technology you use, the more high tech you place in the way of high touch.

3. Focus on Creating a Trusting Relationship

Ironically, paradoxically, the longer you take to establish a trusting relationship, the more quickly you will acquire high-quality business.

Too many professionals want to waltz in and depart with a contract in their arms. It's not in the cards. If you think of the hang tens discussed earlier, you may be able to achieve a faster relationship with them because of their predisposition to try new things rapidly, but a relationship is required, nonetheless.

4. Stop Abandoning the Buyer

Here are two things you *never* need to do:

1. Go out and gather data for a proposal on your own.

2. Go out and meet people because the buyer asks you to do so.

If you're dealing with a legitimate economic buyer, you have everyone who's required to create a quality proposal in the room: you and the buyer. If the buyer insists that you talk to others for "background," immediately set a date for the two of you to debrief once you've done that and reestablish your partnership.

Always inform the buyer that others are likely to be threatened by the kind of change you're proposing (or the buyer is requesting), and that the decision is probably a strategic one that the buyer should be making independent of tactical people.

Listen Up!
There is a reason that the buyer is talking to you. The buyer is interested to some degree. That's a plus. Don't mess it up.

---

5. Don't Provide or Accept Arbitrary Alternatives

When the buyer says, "We'd like you to give us a proposal for a three-day, off-site leadership workshop," your only reply should be, "Why?" The buyer has provided an alternative for you to fill. But what's the objective? Why shouldn't you examine the goal before being part of the route?

Similarly, don't lead with your methodology: "What you need is our six-step Accelerated Sales System (ASS)." The client may need only Steps 3 and 6, or a seventh step as well, or none at all. Ascertain the real need and the desired end result, and work backward from there.

Hundreds of thousands of consultants have lost billions of dollars because they've either accepted a completely unilateral client request or tried to fulfill a legitimate request with an ideology—a fixed methodology.

I'll conclude this chapter and this last topic about allowing the buyer to buy by addressing nonbuyers and nonclients. How do you allow them to "buy into" your worth and value and spread the word for you while offering contacts?

These people are most often

- Professional acquaintances (accountants, doctors, lawyers)
- Social acquaintances (friends or people with shared interests)
- Association colleagues (trade and professional associations)
- Civic colleagues (those on commissions, boards, and task forces)
- Interested others (people who know of your work or buy your products)

In the same manner as with client buyers, you have to make manifest to these people the extent of your results. Don't focus on what you do, *focus on what you achieve*. It's far more powerful to say, "I create individual growth and autonomy" than "I coach managers to think for themselves."

Clients and nonclients alike will "buy" your quality and reputation and be willing to spread them to their circle of friends and colleagues when you follow these simple parameters. You should be striving for these ends in your revenue and referral goals.

You'll know you are successful when referrals are provided when you request them, that you are very successful when they are virtually all top quality and personally introduced; and that you are extremely successful when they come without prompting, being proactively suggested by your contact.

That's how you create annuity business. Now, how do you create annuity business that keeps expanding?

CHAPTER 3

EXPANDED BUSINESS

WHY MORE, NOT LESS, IS BETTER FOR THE CLIENT

WHY NO GOOD DEED (PROJECT) SHOULD GO UNREWARDED (EXPANDED)

A hugely important route for referrals is internal in those organizations that are large enough to support multiple projects (which is why, for example, the small business market is so difficult—you have to continually bring new clients on board). This route is the Interstate Highway of referral travel.

One of the methods I've used successfully to make seven figures as a solo practitioner is to work with large organizations that can support continual (and often concurrent) projects. The reasons that this is such fertile ground for referrals include

- Internal buyers can observe the results and value of your work firsthand within their culture.
- The referral system is "hard wired"—that is, buyers are spending time with one another in company meetings, at meals, on trips, and so on.

- You develop an "insider" knowledge of the company and its culture that provides an instant understanding of its needs and challenges.

- There is an intrinsic (and often extrinsic) belief that the investment in your services should be leveraged in future engagements.

- It would require a Herculean effort by another consultant or consulting firm to dislodge you or to introduce a competitive offering because of your entrenched position.

This latter point is crucial. In the military, it's a basic belief that three times the numbers of an entrenched force are required if an attacker is to have any chance of success in dislodging that force. You have a big advantage being behind the stone wall or inside the gates.

My dictum "think of the fourth sale first" means that you should be continually searching for referrals *within your own clients and within your own immediate buyer's purview*.

As you can see in Figure 3.1, there is a "ring" of expected and unexpected referral sources around most buyers. You should diligently list and pursue these sources, since they will vary somewhat from client to client. In setting priorities, I would always pursue the buyer's peers first if there are any who are in a position to purchase your services.

Not all routes in all clients make sense, of course. Here's a quick way to determine whom to pursue with the most energy, assuming you're convinced that the person is a true economic buyer.

1. *Trusting relationship.* Can you develop (or have you already developed) a trusting relationship with the prospect? Has the existing buyer made inroads for

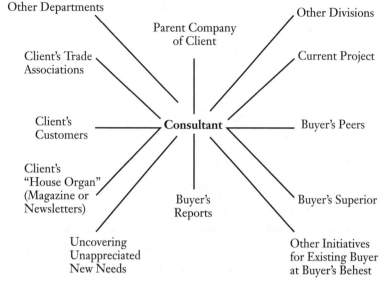

Figure 3.1   Internal Referral Routes

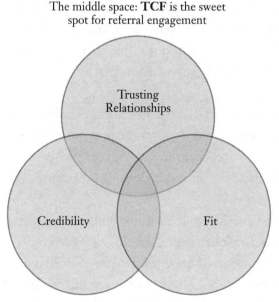

Figure 3.2   Setting Priorities for Internal Referrals

you? Is the person accessible (as opposed to traveling 85 percent of the time)?

2. *Fit.* Are your services appropriate for the needs and issues facing the prospect? Does the prospect require special expertise (financial, technical, and so on) that you don't possess and/or in which you have no interest?

3. *Credibility.* Is the prospect aware of or amenable to understanding your expertise in his or her context? Although you may be quite adept in strategy formulation, for example, if what you've done for your current buyer is sales development, the prospect might not understand your further capabilities.

If you have a trusting relationship and a good fit, but no credibility, then you don't have the "guarantee" and assurance that the prospect requires; if you have a trusting relationship and credibility, but not the fit, then you lack the right tool kit; and if you have credibility and fit, but not a trusting relationship, then you're no better positioned than an external consultant who has never worked within that organization. In other words, you've forfeited your internal referral advantage (see Figure 3.2).

The bottom line is that successful projects in high-potential organizations should always carry the additional value to you of an inside track on future (or concurrent) work. But you have to analyze the situation, establish priorities, and take the appropriate steps.

My estimate is that for most solo practitioners and boutique firms, *total* client relationships range from two months to nine months. Most of these practices are forced to create at least 50 percent or more in new business annually. But consultants who appreciate and follow this referral advice average between a *year and five years* with a single client, and need to bring in only about 20 percent of new (unreferred) business a year (which is a healthy combination in any case).

I've had six-, ten-, and twelve-year relationships with quite a few clients, and two- to four-year relationships with most. That is a huge difference in terms of lowered cost of acquisition, higher annual revenues, and still further referral business outside of the organization.

"IF YOU THINK THIS IS GOOD": DEMONSTRATING LEVERAGE

There is a particular mindset that you need if you are to gain referrals and dramatically expand your business. I would describe it like this: *You have tremendous value to deliver to your clients. You would be remiss if you didn't take every opportunity to inform them of, demonstrate, and expand that value so that you are benefiting the client as much as possible.*

I'm not talking about revenue or quotas or sales or "closing." This mindset is a very different starting point. If you're absolutely convinced of your value and your impact on clients, then you'll want to assertively seek opportunities to provide it. You'll never be reluctant or reserved.

Once the client appreciates your work, you will have that much more of an opportunity to expand it. That's not a risk, not "pushy," not inappropriate. It's the natural thing to do.

This is the central point of leveraging your existing business for referrals to gain more business—to spread your value. When I began in this business, I honestly thought that consultants were failing because they were undercapitalized. I even wrote about this.

I'm always surprised by how stupid I was two weeks ago.

I was completely wrong. The main reason for consultants failing is *lack of self-esteem*. They (yes, *you*) often believe that they are not good enough, that they don't belong, or that they'll be "found out." But I learned long ago that common sense is in short supply and highly valuable. (About 90 percent of the time, I validate what the client already knows. Only 10 percent of the time do I introduce new and unprecedented approaches.)

Listen Up!
The first sale is always to yourself. If you're not absolutely convinced of the value you bring to the client, why should the client be convinced?

Here is a test of your self-esteem. Be honest; no one is scoring you other than you:

1. Do you talk, dress, and behave as a peer of the buyer, or do you take the role of a subordinate, a vendor, or a mendicant?

2. Will you boldly suggest courses of action that involve more work for you on the grounds that the client's improvement is so strong?

3. Do you vacillate and review your written communications to the client repeatedly so as to strike "just the right tone"?

4. Will you honestly and readily critique the buyer when he is not meeting his goals?

5. Do you speak up at meetings even if your point of view isn't shared by the majority?

6. Can you separate principle from taste, and will you fight to preserve the former while going along with others on the latter?

7. Do you take prudent risks in order to move things along?

8. Do you allow the client to dictate how you should consult or coach?

9. Are you resilient when you undergo a setback or defeat?

High self-esteem key:

1. Yes.

2. Yes.

3. No.

4. Yes.

5. Yes.

6. Yes.

7. Yes.

8. No.

9. Yes.

For high self-esteem, *you need a perfect score!*

There's a difference between high self-esteem and high efficacy. The latter is the condition of being good at something. The former is the condition of having high self-worth, whether you perform well or not.

In Figure 3.3, high efficacy and high self-esteem are ideal. If you simply have high efficacy, but you don't feel worthy (upper right), you feel like an imposter. And those people who have huge self-esteem but don't perform well we often call "empty suits" or "big hats, no cattle." If you have neither, then you're alienated.

I've actually had consultants ask me why a key buyer would ever listen to them! I can't give them an answer, because at that

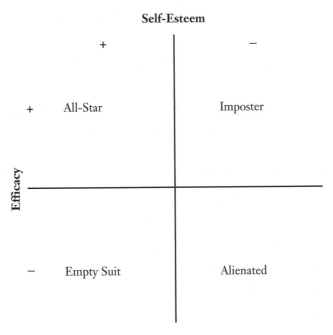

Figure 3.3   Self-Esteem and Efficacy

point I don't feel like listening to them. That's why the mind-set I first described is so vital.

Thus, those who are in the upper left quadrant have no qualms about saying to the buyer, "If you think this project went well, wait until you hear about the next one I'm going to propose!" After all, that's the least you can do for a key client—improve her condition still further.

Here are some situations (we'll discuss the exact language later in the chapter) in which you should exploit the value you bring to the client:

- You hear of someone who is interested in the current results, and you ask your buyer to introduce you and validate the results.

- You observe or learn of a situation that you can demonstrably improve, even though it doesn't relate to your current project.

- You develop ideas that can be of tremendous benefit to this client, based on your growing knowledge and familiarity.

- You introduce "best practices" from other clients that can also serve this client well.

- You see logical extensions and expansions of the current project.

How many of these are you routinely searching for? Are they a part of the diagnostics that you apply during client engagements? To what extent are you allowing the client to take advantage of still more value?!

None of us is successful because we correct weaknesses. We are successful largely because we build on strengths. There is no greater accelerator than a positive, visible, dramatic result that you can then leverage to create more such high-potential situations. But you have to be willing to acknowledge your own value, actively engage the buyer in the evaluation, and blow your own horn.

Finally, always keep in mind that the people you are dealing with have professional colleagues in other organizations, vendor relationships, trade and professional association memberships, community connections, extended family, and other connections who may be superb referrals for you.

I hope you're beginning to appreciate that the sheer number of potential referrals is vast, diverse, and omnipresent. You have to make a point of hunting them down and seeking them out. In other words, you have to be willing to move in many directions simultaneously.

MOVING UP, DOWN, INSIDE, OUTSIDE, AND ALL AROUND

Seeking referrals is more sophisticated than a scavenger hunt but less scientific than GPS. Visualize yourself as being on an intelligent exploration of familiar territory, sort of like moving on and off known trails with a good map.

You can still get lost, but if you pay attention, you should arrive at your intended destination. Figure 3.4 shows you a sample.

Figure 3.4 puts you in the middle, working internally for a client, with a variety of paths to choose for finding people and/or creating exposure for your value.

I was introduced once to the members of a top client team by their boss, who had hired me, who had used my help in a prior company, and who, himself, had once been a consultant

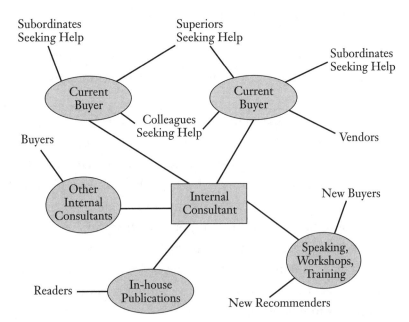

Figure 3.4   Moving in Many Directions

in a former life. He opened with, "Alan is a consultant who, like any good consultant, will work closely with us until, like some incurable disease, he has taken root in our systems and we will not be able to get rid of him."

That brought some nervous laughter (including my own), but I understood his point. Good consultants want to do such good work and meet so many potential buyers that they spread their tentacles throughout the organization seeking sustenance. This is because my mindset is that the organization needs my value, as discussed earlier, not because I'm "searching for business" or "trying to reach revenue quotas."

In your calendar, or diary, or Filofax®, or cocktail coaster (whatever you use for critical reminders), you should note the following potential referral sources and check off whether you've inquired about them. If you don't discipline yourself, you'll tend to overlook sources. Feel free to copy this right out of these pages. Note how many of these sources there are, and that you cannot afford to overlook any of them in any client.

Potential Referral Sources to Be Sought

Buyer peers	Buyer superiors
Buyer subordinates	Client vendors
People in parent organization	People in subsidiaries
Professional colleagues	Acquaintances and friends
Client's customers	Trade associations
Regulatory groups	Media contacts

My estimation is that it is about 20 times more difficult to bring in new business than it is to develop repeat and referral business. It also costs five or six times more in money and time. Think about it. Asking for a referral or another project within a client takes little time and zero investment. Trying to unearth a new client—to turn a cold lead into a warm prospect and then a hot client—is laborious and expensive in terms of trips, time, and managing the process.

Thus, your hunt for referrals is an excellent investment with a significant ROI.

Listen Up!
You never know where your next referral is coming from. Neither you nor I can be that smart. Consequently, look for them everywhere, all the time, with great energy.

I like to look at referrals with this kind of stratification:

1. *Direct buyer to buyer.* No matter which of the previous categories you choose, your buyer provides a direct and personal introduction to a peer who can write a check for your value if you're convincing. It doesn't get any better than this.

2. *Buyer to nonbuyer.* The buyer gives you a powerful reference, but to someone who can't buy. In this case, you have to work your way up to the new buyer. This can be aided by the fact that a buyer gave you the original reference. As a preventive, it's helpful to let your current buyer know *exactly* what kind of person you desire an introduction to.

3. *Nonbuyer to buyer.* This isn't all that unusual when you have highly effective staff people who are in the position of finding resources for their own line clients. Enlightened human resource functions can serve this purpose. In large companies, once you prove your worth, many staff people will fall all over themselves to introduce you because you're a known entity, and the positive fallout will be bestowed on everyone involved.

4. *Nonbuyer to nonbuyer.* These are tough, and I advise you to put them at the rearmost of your back burner. But they can be useful, since they prevent you from being a complete stranger, and you can rely on some familiar faces. Whatever you do, don't allow yourself to be trapped in the lower-level strata, because your peers should be at a higher level.

When you're looking for referrals from nonclient sources—e.g., club members, professional providers, civic connections, family, friends, and social networks—always try to specify *who the ideal individual for you to meet is in terms of title, responsibility, and so forth.* Otherwise, you'll be faced with a great many referrals to follow up with, but that might be largely futile.

Before we move on, a few words about social media platforms: with the exception of specific personal services, such as insurance or real estate, the social media are not great places to obtain references (or to pursue them). Of course people have gained referrals and clients there, but it's not frequent that it's a good investment of your valuable time. (After all, you could find $100 on the street tomorrow morning, but I doubt that you'll quit your job and plan to support your family that way in the future.) There are too many people collecting real and virtual business cards these days.

You're better off with a personal appeal and a personal visit to both solicit a referral and follow up on it. Most people on social media don't have contacts so much as a "collection" of people who like to develop lists of quantitative names without qualitative impact.

E-mail in one-dimensional, the phone is two-dimensional, and being present is three-dimensional. Referrals are by far best in 3-D.

LANGUAGE TEMPLATE

In the next several pages, I'm hoping to provide some practical language that can revolutionize your ability to gain referrals, expand your business, and extend relationships. First, please consider this sequence:

Language——Discussion——Relationships——Business

Language controls discussion, which controls relationships, which in turn control business. I'm a "purist" on language because I've always appreciated its profound impact. Don't scoff at the difference between "infer" and "imply"[1] or between "denote" and "connote" or between "prone" and "supine"; they have nuanced meanings that increase your ability to communicate.

The discussion that results from your language will create a relationship that, ideally, will establish you as a peer and trusted advisor of the buyer. That relationship will then determine the type, scope, and nature of the business that ensues.

Thus, it all begins with the words you choose.

Listen Up!
What words, phrases, and expressions have most influenced you? Why? Remember that impact when you choose the language you intend to apply in your discussions with buyers.

From what follows, choose the techniques that are most comfortable for you. Modify them as necessary to suit your style and environment. But bear in mind that I've developed and cap-

---

[1] The speaker implies; the listener infers. They are not interchangeable, unless you believe that Facebook is Shakespeare and Wikipedia is *Webster's Unabridged.*

tured these from nearly three decades of consulting and coaching work.

Gaining Agreement to Discuss a Topic

You will want to broach the subject of referrals (or anything else, such as an overdue fee or a request for more participation) with a suitable opening. I've coined the term *rhetorical permission*, which looks like this:

- "May I raise an important issue at this point?"
- "May I take just a minute to review something we've discussed earlier?"
- "Could we discuss an issue on my agenda at this point?"
- "If we've finished on this subject, may I suggest a new one that's a high priority?"
- "Could I take two minutes to discuss one more issue?"

As you can see, not one of these will result in a "no" or "not now" answer, especially if you are in a peer-to-peer, trusting relationship with the buyer. They are mere rhetorical contrivances to prepare the buyer for the topic. They present a nice segue, and they create an automatic "permission" to proceed.

Citing the Issue

You now want to raise the issue of referrals directly and professionally. If you've laid the proper framework, then you're merely revisiting the subject at this point:

- "Do you recall that at the outset of our work together, I raised the issue of referrals, and you agreed to provide some at an appropriate time during the project?"

- "On occasion, I've alluded to the great importance of referrals in my work, and I'd like to pursue them with you at this juncture, given the success we're seeing with this project."

- "It's an appropriate time to discuss referrals, and I have some suggestions for whom some of them might be."

- "The sixth action point we had agreed upon was to discuss referrals three-quarters of the way through the project, and that day has come!"

- "Referrals are the coinage of my particular realm, and so I am diligent in trying to develop these from outstanding clients such as you."

Asking

If you don't ask, you don't get. (Professional fund-raisers actually call this "the Ask.") The language should be concise and clear:

- "Can you offer me three names of people who, like you, could greatly benefit from this type of value, and would you be willing to introduce me to them?"

- "At this point, which people in your communities would be most appropriate for introductions for me and the value of my work?"

- "I've noted six people who may be strong candidates to consider this type of project for their own operations. I'd love to get your advice about that and, if they are appropriate, your introduction to them."

- "Who is there outside of the company and beyond those of whom we've already spoken who may be ideal beneficiaries of this value and development?"
- "What three names would be the priority contacts to consider this type of project and outcome for their own operations?"

Deflecting

You will see resistance or forgetfulness or procrastination at times (although the stronger your relationship with the buyer, the less you should encounter this). Here are samples of resistance and rebuttals:

- "I wasn't really prepared to discuss this yet."
- *"I understand. I've brought some names to get your reaction, and perhaps we can build upon them."*
- "I'm a bit uncomfortable that others may think I've sent a salesperson after them."
- *"That's not how you see me. If you think there is value in what I can do for them, then you're doing them a favor, not creating an imposition!"*
- "Why don't I approach them for you? Let me know what you'd like me to say or to give to them."
- *"That's not fair to anyone. I can't allow you to do my marketing for me, and they will inevitably have questions about my approaches that you won't be able to answer."*
- "Let me give you their assistants and human resource support staff."
- *"That's not going to work, just as it wouldn't have worked with you! Their assistants, with the best of intentions, will try to shield the boss."*

- "They are probably traveling or extremely busy at the moment."
- *"As are you and I, but we have to start somewhere. I promise to use discretion and would never 'hound' anyone whom you recommend."*

You can see that setting up the request, making the request, and deflecting innocent procrastination about the request are easily handled using the proper language. And always give this option:

- "Ideally, I would love a personal introduction at a meeting, or by phone, or by e-mail. But if that's not possible, I'd like permission to use your name and our work together when I contact this person."

Try to never accept, "You can have this name, but don't mention me." Find out why there is that reluctance to be involved.

Remember, this is a three-way favor, and with that attitude, there should really be no reservation about providing a referral to someone else who would be demonstrably improved by doing business with you. Find the cause of the reluctance when you encounter it, and deal with the reason (for example, the person doesn't like salespeople to call) so that you can provide the appropriate assurances.

WHEN YOU HIT THE CEILING, AND HOW TO GO THROUGH IT

There are occasions when you seem to have reached the end of the referral chain. The buyers have no more names, you've exhausted the various internal and external avenues discussed earlier, and the mine's ore is seriously depleted.

The smaller the business, the more likely it is that this will happen. But it will also occur when

- Your buyer moves (transfers, retires, is recruited elsewhere, or is fired).
- You've been as diligent as you can, but you want to stop short of stalking the buyer.
- Company policy prohibits it.
- The buyer's personal preferences discourage it (for example, a very timid person who does not like to "impose" on others).
- A referral objected because either the buyer or you calculated incorrectly as to the "fit" and receptivity.
- There are confidentiality issues.

So there will be times when you seem to have hit the "ceiling" and there is no higher place to proceed. Before ending this chapter, I'd like to give you some advice on how to prevent this and/or deal with it contingently, since I think at this point you've come to appreciate how much value a client provides for your referral system and future business.

Listen Up!
If you know that some adverse conditions may emerge, you're negligent if you don't consider them and implement steps to prevent them or mitigate their effects.

---

1. Develop a Multitude of Referral Sources

Don't rely solely on your buyer. Develop these people as well:

- Nonbuyers with whom you implement and interact, who can provide introductions to (or at least names of) true buyers elsewhere
- Prospective buyers in the organization with whom you are not doing business but who are accessible
- Nonclient personnel you meet in the course of your business

Hint: Act as if you're doing a 360-degree assessment of the buyer. The people you would include in that assessment circle are those who may constitute additional reference sources!

2. Institutionalize Your Work

Document your work thoroughly so that it has permanence beyond the buyer's memory or your mutual discussions. You can do this by

- Providing interviews for internal client publications
- Providing learning aids and job performance tools that are tangible and enduring
- Creating newsletters, CDs, downloads, videos, and so forth that maintain your contributions very visibly

3. Create and Maintain Ongoing Relationships

You can "stay in the loop" by

- Providing electronic or hard-copy newsletters
- Exchanging holiday cards
- Joining organizations that the client belongs to

- Serving as a reference for the client as appropriate
- Remembering key anniversaries or activities

4. Offer Complimentary Services

Sometimes it's better to invest in your future with a client than to try to make money immediately. ("Think of the fourth sale first.") There is nothing wrong with

- Offering to speak at a company conference or event
- Performing an "audit" on progress semiannually
- Acting as a "sounding board" for your buyer if a critical event develops
- Appearing as a guest or observer at company functions, celebrations, and special events

5. Join Appropriate Trade and Professional Organizations

Especially if your client is already a member, you may be able to join as a member, an affiliate, or simply a guest to remain connected with your client and important others in the industry or profession. This might include

- Serving on professional panels
- Writing in the professional literature and on websites
- Learning the present and future "hot buttons" of the industry
- Meeting the "movers and shakers" in the business (typically, *any* board member is a potentially great referral source)
- Reconnecting with your client in relevant circumstances

During my career, I consulted with dozens of pharmaceutical, newspaper, and banking clients concurrently. That's because I was receiving referrals *within the industry from my clients*. The competitive taboos we often hear about are not borne out in reality. I was always careful to alert my clients about who else I was working with (I could hardly claim, as a large firm could, "We have a different team on that!"), and I never once received an objection over 25 years!

In fact, in most cases, these were the suggestions:

- "I used to work at Acme, and they could use you. Contact my old boss, Harry."
- "My sister-in-law was just promoted over at Universal, and she desperately needs help. I think you'd be perfect. I told her you'd be calling."
- "I met someone at a trade association meeting, and his internal people are not getting the job done. He needs a good consultant, fast. Mention my name; I may need the favor returned some time."
- "We're going to be getting into a joint venture over there, so I want to send you over to our initial contacts now."

Even when you seem to have hit the ceiling, you can find ways to continue to generate referrals. Most consultants give up too early. They give up when they're told, "I just can't think of anyone." (This is like giving up when a prospect says, "We just don't have any money." Of course she has money; she just doesn't see you as a priority destination for it!) You've gone far beyond that here, but I'm telling you not to give up, even when you may believe you're at the end of the road.

Let's look now at how to exploit this "platinum standard" for developing new business.

CHAPTER 4

THE PLATINUM STANDARD

ASKING FOR REFERRALS IS DOING THREE PEOPLE A FAVOR

THE MENTALITY OF VALUE, NOT SALES

I spoke earlier of having a sincere, constant belief in the value that you provide, and that this value should be your driving force in finding business (as opposed to quotas, or revenue, or numbers of clients). If you believe that, ongoing referral business, at any given time, is doing three people a favor:

1. Your existing client, who is providing value to someone else
2. That third party, who will benefit from that value
3. You

Thus, Hal Mapes, whose story was given at the beginning of this book, was exponentially helping people throughout the year. The third party is usually new; the referring party may be the same or may be new; but you are always the same. So this three-way good deal always has you as a constant beneficiary.

Thus, the math can look like this:

- You have 50 client and nonclient referral sources.
- You ask each for three names.
- Of the 150 names you receive, you create business with 10 percent, or15.
- You have increased your client base by 30 percent!
- If you average even $10,000 per engagement, you've increased your revenue by $150,000; if you average $50,000, then you've increased it by $750,000!

This may sound phantasmagorical, but that's because most of us put our exclusive emphasis on business and revenue from clients and not on referral potential. Moreover, we tend to ignore referral potential with nonclients.

One of the keys to keep in mind is what I call the value distance (see Figure 4.1). The value distance is that progression from what the client thinks he wants to what he really needs. For example, "wanting" a sales training session may actually be an indication that the client needs to reduce the attrition of existing clients and the resulting need to constantly find new ones. The "want" of a strategy retreat may be an indicator of a need for better coordination among operating units.

The more you satisfy client needs, the larger the scope of your projects, the greater the impact, and the higher the fees. That will encourage more and higher-quality referrals. And, for that matter, the more your clients demonstrate that their needs are being met by providing you with referrals, the more quantity and quality you'll receive in that realm.

The point is to maintain that three-way benefit. The more quality the buyer sees in providing your value to others, the more and better referrals will ensue. Don't make this about you; *make it about the buyer!*

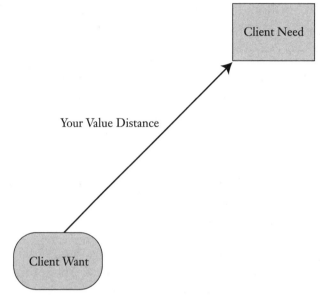

Figure 4.1   Value Distance

CASE STUDY: The Barbecue

A woman I was coaching told me that her best friend lived next door, and that her friend's husband, whom she didn't know well at all, was an executive at a downtown bank that would be ideal for her consulting work.

They both attended the woman's neighborhood Fourth of July barbecue, and the woman found herself talking to the husband at length for the first time.

"I was hopeless," she confessed. "What was I going to do, ask him whom I should see at his bank for my services over a hot dog?"

"No, but you could have said, 'This isn't the time or the place, but can I stop by to see you next week to ask you a question about my work?' How could he have refused?"

Think about the times you have automatically—without thinking twice—provided someone with the name of your doctor, accountant, mechanic, designer, ticket broker, gardener, travel agent, and so forth. Why did you do that without reservation? Why didn't you say, "Let me think about it"? Why didn't you hesitate or worry?

I'll tell you why:

- You weren't worried about whether the people you were recommending were good. You knew they were and were convinced of it.

- You weren't worried about whether they would be overburdened by the added business. You figured they could handle that.

- You weren't worried that you would now receive less of their time. You're a good patient/client/customer, and you were confident that you would be treated as well as always.

- You were confident that the professional would appreciate your endorsement.

- You might even believe you'd derive some benefit from the referral—a gift certificate, faster response, priority on lists, a return referral for your business, and so forth.

- You believed the person you were referring to these people was a legitimate prospect for them and not a waste of their time.

- You believed you might derive a benefit from the person you were referring, in gratitude for her having been placed in touch with a consummate professional through your auspices.

I could go on, but I think you get my drift. What can you do to create that same "unconscious" recommending of you to others? How can you be the doctor, architect, dentist, or stylist in my previous examples?

First, you have to do extremely fine work. Not just "good" work, but stellar work.

Second, you have to make it clear that you are eager to accept referral work and, in fact, will often request it.

Third, you have to provide some positive reinforcement to the referral source. I'm not talking about a bribe or kickback or some other lagniappe, and I'll provide ideas at the conclusion of this chapter, but something that manifests appreciation.

Fourth, you must arrange for the *new* client referred to you to get back to the referral source and demonstrate gratitude for putting the two of you together. *Nothing* will stimulate referrals like being congratulated for the quality of the connection by earlier referrals!

POSITIONING THE REQUEST AND FOLLOWING UP

There are, of course, good times and bad times to ask for referral names. For example, bad times would include

- In the restroom
- During a meeting with others
- Calling at home late at night
- During a fire drill
- When you're being told your project is failing
- While the buyer is on vacation

You get the idea. You have to choose your moments.

Strategically

My best results have been generated when I set up the future request at the time the proposal is accepted, and then make the request about *two-thirds of the way through the initial project.*

It's not a good idea to talk about referrals prior to securing your project. So the acceptance of the proposal is the trigger point for beginning that conversation. Once you're thanking the buyer for the business and arranging the initial implementation, you can plant the seed with:

"Once we're both delighted with the progress of the project, I'll be asking you for referrals, since my clients are my best source of new clients. Is that okay at some point?"

I've never had anyone say no, but if anyone were to say, "Our policy is against that," or "I have some reservations," that's the best time to find out!

The reasons I recommend making the request about two-thirds of the way through the project duration are

- There should be ample progress to delight the buyer.
- You have a good idea of potential referral sources and targets.
- You are still *present* and visiting the client.[1]
- You have time to follow up and fine-tune the request.

Tactically

You have some options when you are ready to actually make your "ask" (as the fund-raisers say). There is no royal road, but here's an express lane:

[1] Absence, in this business, does not make the heart grow fonder; it makes people forget.

1. Use a scheduled meeting, not a special meeting you set up just to acquire referrals. You should be scheduling regular debriefing and status reports anyway.

2. Ideally, use a face-to-face meeting, not a phone meeting, and never e-mail. E-mail is one-dimensional, the phone is two-dimensional, and a personal meeting is three-dimensional. Only the last maximizes your ability to persuade, influence, and clarify.

3. Advise the client that you have an agenda issue for that meeting and work it into the time frame. So, if you have an hour, use 40 minutes for your debriefing and the buyer's questions, and then 20 minutes for your referral requests.

Then you can use this type of language: "I mentioned at the outset of the project that if we're both delighted with the progress, I'd like to ask you for referrals for my work. Given our conversation this morning, it's clear that we're both delighted, and we're now in the 'home stretch' of the work. Here are some criteria for the best referrals for me. Whom would you recommend I be seeking?"

Note that you've worked this into a scheduled meeting about success. You can always choose not to ask if something unexpected surfaces during the meeting. It's very useful to suggest

- Criteria for the ideal referral (for example, those holding P&L responsibility, sales vice presidents, small business owners, and so forth)

- Specific names you've come up with (since you've been there this long into the project): Tom Smith, Jane Jones

Finally, two responses are likely, so be prepared:

Response 1: "Sure, I'll recommend these people."
Your next comment: "Thank you. Would you be willing to introduce me?"

Response 2: "I'm not sure. I'll have to give it some more thought."
Your next comment: "I understand. We're due to meet again on the twenty-fifth; can we agree that we'll discuss the specific names at that time?"

So there's your express route: you've set up the expectation and then delivered on the request under optimal conditions. While it doesn't always work out perfectly, *the key is to establish the overall structure and expectations that are most in your favor.* That makes it easier to deal with exceptions and resistance.

Listen Up!
You control the impetus, direction, and speed of your referral stream. You must be assertive and directive to be effective.

In terms of nonbusiness referrals (from all those other great sources such as professional colleagues, friends, club members, and so forth), you should periodically remind people of your value *and changes in that value.*

Mention to your dentist that you've just created a new community for strategy officers. Offer an "enrichment night" at your club to share your new approaches to stress reduction and life balance. Over drinks with your banking executive neighbor, mention that you've just helped cut attrition at a major financial institution through an empowerment model.

Strategically

Stratify your contacts so that you're keenly aware of which represent the highest referral potential for you (irrespective of how well you know them). Arrange for opportunities to be in their company. (Again, personal contact is the key; you're wasting your time with e-mail or phone calls.) Develop a familiarity with them and, where possible, offer them value—a referral for them, an idea, an opportunity that has nothing to do with you.

In other words, arrange for comfortable access.

Tactically

After you've developed a positive degree of familiarity and ideally have offered the other person some value, clearly and concisely discuss the value you provide and ask her advice on whom she recommends you should be pursuing. Never try to "sell" to her, personally. Rather, get her advice on whom to approach and, once she gives you names, ask if she would be comfortable making an introduction. Most people will be amenable to such requests *because they have made them of others in the past.* In the worst case, they'll decline.

Positioning costs you nothing, allows you to maximize your chances of success, and creates a plan that you can follow no less than the plan for your project's success with that client.

PRIMING THE PUMP (NOT TAKING NO FOR AN ANSWER)

Once you're past the first major hurdle—being willing to ask for referrals and having the tools to do so—the next hurdle that trips up most consultants is the client refusing. The client says, "Sorry," or, "Not now," or, "I'll think about it," or, "No," and we pack our tents and slink off into the night.

Two keys here:

1. How many times in your life have you responded to a "no" (or even a "later") by simply giving up? Did you do that as a child? As a competitive teenager? As a new person in a job? Have you achieved the level of success, happiness, and contribution you have today—no matter what they are—simply by accepting a refusal as your fate? I doubt it. Our human wiring doesn't provide for a collapse when facing resistance; it provides for investigation of how to circumvent, navigate, or blast through resistance.

2. A "no" is not a finality, just as time and money are not resources, they are priorities. When people claim they are saying no because they have no money or no time, they are being disingenuous at best and lying at worst. They *do* have money, and they *do* have time (the lights are on, the mortgage is being paid, and they have the time to tell you no), but they have decided for the moment not to give them to you because there are other priorities that are more important to them than you. That means you can't address the *resource* issue to change this; you must address the *priority* issue!

Not only can't you accept resistance or delay, but you can't allow yourself to believe the validity of the resistance. Here are some internal beliefs or values you must embrace to avoid falling over these hurdles:

The Irresistible Value Principle

You have to believe that your value is so important that it should not be denied to others, and that your client (or potential referral source) is the entry point to the road that will help you reach a multitude of people who can use that value. Doctors don't accept a patient's "no" when they tell the patient that he has to take certain medicine, and that he avoids exercise and diet regimens at his own risk.

The first sale is to yourself.

The Concurrent, Multiple-Win Principle

Your referral source must understand and embrace the fact that she is doing a favor for the third parties, not merely for you, and therefore is providing an investment for herself when this kind of valuable offer is reciprocated. If people think they're doing this *merely for you*, they will not be invested. If they believe they are doing it for a valued third party, they will feel like a Samaritan. But if they feel that they are also investing in their own future well-being, they will also be motivated by a return on that investment.

Referrals benefit everyone involved.

The Reconnaissance Principle

We've discussed preparing your referral source for the fact that you'll be asking, and building the request into a favorable meeting situation. During the course of the first two-thirds of your project, keep a list of highly likely new business sources within and outside the client. Check out the landscape. Be prepared to "prime the pump" by identifying targets with your referral source in the event your buyer doesn't come up with sources for you.

Familiarize yourself with the objective before you arrive.

The Resistance Preparatory Principle

There is a finite number of resistance sources:

- I'm not prepared; I've been busy; I need more time.
- I'll have to check; I'm not sure the people I have in mind are willing.
- I'm uncomfortable imposing on these people.
- I can't think of anyone.

There may be variations of these, but if you know the primary probable causes of procrastination and resistance, it's negligent not to prepare for them. Obviously, you need to be prepared to demonstrate the value to all three partners (the referral source, the third party, and you), you must have names to suggest, and you must give examples of how this is a normal, collegial action under most conditions.

Never be surprised by resistance.

> **Listen Up!**
> *Here's a great retort to "I just can't think of anyone appropriate." You reply, "That's what I first hear from about 90 percent of my best referrals! Let me give you some guidelines, and the names will flow . . ."* Don't let them escape; paint them into the picture.*

Think about those times you would have loved to have secured referrals but did not. What were the causes? (You can apply the same rationale to projects you bid on but didn't acquire!) Was the failure the client's fault or your fault?

There may be legitimate occasions when it's not possible to obtain referrals, *but my experience shows that, if you have diligence and preparation, those happen only about 5 percent of the time!*

That's right, 5 percent. What's your current success rate? If it's less than 95 percent, then I can assure you that a great deal of the problem is with you, not your referral sources.

As you can see in Figure 4.2, *you* control the percentage of time you'll be successful. If you never ask at all, some referrals will trickle in because your work is good and you are cited. If you ask with preparation, diligence, and confidence, you'll acquire referrals almost every time.

The problem is that people don't "prime the pump" and feel they're doing well with the mere trickle.

If you disagree with me that referrals are as valuable as or even more valuable than the immediate client revenue in the longer term, then you ignore these opportunities and personal preventive actions at your own risk, and at the cost of your long-term business success.

The pump isn't dry. You're simply not applying the right technique and the right force.

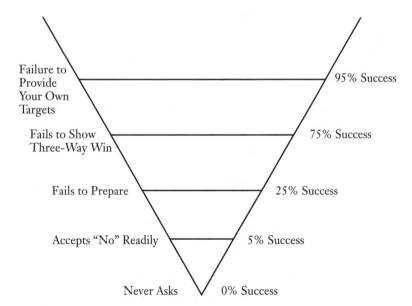

Figure 4.2 Overcoming Personal Referral Limitations

APPROACHING THE THIRD PARTY IRRESISTIBLY

I've been pretty much exclusively discussing the referral source to this point, so let's proceed to talk about the new prospect. (What to call this person? Referrent? Referrit? Referee?)

I'll simply use "referral."

The referral can be approached in three basic ways:

1. An introduction from your referral source. This may be
   - In person, in either office, off-site, at a social event, and so forth.
   - By phone, with you on the call or not on the call.
   - By e-mail, with you copied on the e-mail or not.
   - By hard-copy letter, with a copy to you or not.
   - Through a third party, e.g., "When you run into Jim next week, mention to him that a woman named Joan Reynolds may be calling at my suggestion."
2. Permission for you to contact the referral directly, using your referral source's name. This may include
   - Meeting the person at an event or during the course of work and introducing yourself.
   - Calling the individual.
   - E-mailing the individual.
   - Sending hard-copy mail to the individual.
   - Attempting to contact the individual through a third party, usually an assistant or secretary.
3. Using a name provided to you without permission to use the referral source's name. This would include the same steps as in case 2:

- Meeting the person at an event or during the course of work and introducing yourself.
- Calling the individual.
- E-mailing the individual.
- Sending hard-copy mail to the individual.
- Attempting to contact the individual through a third party, usually an assistant or secretary.

Let's be very clear. The most effective and productive manner in which to approach referrals and secure business is with a direct introduction in person. In fact, the efficacy of the approaches declines as you work down each step and bullet point in my lists, with the most futile being to try to contact a name provided to you without using your referral source, and through an assistant.

In this last case, you have deteriorated to what is in every respect a cold call. You're out of the referral universe, since you could have obtained that name (and no further help, as you have no further help here) from newspapers or random conversations.

Listen Up!
There is a hierarchy of referral contact effectiveness.
Try to stay at the very top of the hierarchy.

If you can achieve a personal introduction, then comport yourself as you would with any new prospect: ascertain that this is a buyer for your value; develop a trusting relationship; gain conceptual agreement on objectives, measures, and value; and provide a proposal with options. The fact that you've been personally introduced by a valued intermediary (for whom you may well have provided excellent value already) should accelerate the trusting relationship aspect of your progression.

I want to focus especially on the conditions that exist when you have been introduced remotely in the first approach: your referral source has sung your praises, and the referral is awaiting (or at least expecting) some contact from you.

First, always keep in mind your next "yes," which is a personal meeting. Don't attempt to sell, pitch, influence, cajole, present, persuade, or otherwise obtain a close in your initial communication, which should always be by phone. *Your sole objective is to gain a personal meeting.*

Tactics:

- If a subordinate, assistant, or gatekeeper, says, "What is this in reference to?" or "I'll give him your message," or "I have the task of scheduling for her," just reply, "I'm sorry, but this is a personal matter relating to a message he received from his colleague, Paul Kirk, which I'm following up on, as promised."

- If the referral says, "Can we discuss this by phone right now?" reply, "Not productively, and not in keeping with my promise to Paul Kirk to provide my personal time for you. Surely there is a 30-minute window, on-site or off, that is convenient for you?"[2]

- Stress that you made a promise to your referral source, that you've provided her with tremendous value, and that you wouldn't normally be pursuing this person, except, "Jane has never failed to give me good advice on whom I should be talking to, and I

[2] Ask for a reasonable amount of time, not an hour and not 10 minutes. If you're effective in the meeting, the referral will either expand the time or agree to meet again for a longer period. The idea is to get in the door.

believe that both of us will find a great deal of value in the meeting, even if it's just for one brief session."

Stress the investment of the referral source in bringing you together, your promise to that person to *personally* provide your time, and the outstanding value that the source feels is appropriate through your intervention.

If you encounter an intermediary by phone, simply leave your phone number and a reference to "the personal message from Paul Kirk that you're following up on." If you encounter voice mail, do the same in a very brief message. Under no circumstances should you get into details or make a pitch. Your sole objective is a personal meeting to begin the process of relationship building.

Here's some additional ammunition. Use this line: "I'll be talking to Paul on Friday, and I'd like to be able to tell him that I was successful in contacting you, as I had promised." Bring in the obligation to the third party to help create urgency.

When you are contacting the referral without that personal introduction, but with permission to use the referral source's name, try these, or some variation:

- "Paul Kirk strongly recommended that I contact you about the work that he and I have been engaged in over the past three months. I don't normally do this, but he assured me that you would be both receptive and appropriate for learning about what we've accomplished."
- "I'm calling at the insistence of Paul Kirk. He rarely suggests I talk to people, but on the few occasions that he does, it's always resulted in a highly valuable relationship."

- "Paul Kirk has asked me to spend 20 minutes with you, personally, with the idea that you'd be able to know in that time whether what we accomplished together also makes sense to you."

You get the idea: make it irresistible. You can also see that you need to avoid at all costs, "I can give you names, but you can't use my name." Anyone can do that. It's like your current client saying, "I can pay you, but not in real money."

HOW TO REWARD AND STIMULATE REFERRAL SOURCES

As with most things in life, care and feeding go a long way toward helping referrals grow and prosper.

First, let's talk about the most obvious kind of reward: monetary. You can give someone a referral fee, provided

- He is not engaged by the referral to find additional help, and he does not choose you and accept your fee under the guise of simply finding a highly reliable resource. In other words, it's unethical for someone to tell his client that he's found a fine resource on an objective basis when, in fact, he's being paid to recommend you.
- He is not a member of an organization (for example, an independent entrepreneur or professional). It is unethical to pay employees of either the referral source or the referral organization for the referral. (Increasingly, it's against companies' policies to offer any kind of emolument or lagniappe to an employee in any form. Even at meals, the company employee is expected to pay and never be paid for by an outsider.)

So, assuming that we're talking about another consultant, coach, or similar professional, here is the referral fee basis I recommend:

- If you've simply been given the name of a legitimate buyer, but no help or inside track to reach that buyer (which makes it, for all intents and purposes, a targeted cold call), I would pay 5 percent of the initial project fee.

- If you're given a name and introduction that gets you into the buyer's office on good terms (whether the introduction is in person or remote, the point is that you were able to get there), I suggest 10 to 15 percent.

- If the other party makes the sale for you, and you merely have to show up and meet the buyer, I recommend 15 to 20 percent. (This can occur when a trusted friend or colleague of the buyer convinces the buyer that you're the best, perhaps a colleague at a club, on a civic committee, or at a neighborhood event.)

You can adjust these to your heart's content, but I feel they are appropriate *for the initial project only*. I would not offer these for renewal business or in perpetuity.

Most of the time, *a thank-you note is sufficient, but there is one better way: reciprocity.*

Listen Up!
When you and others exchange referrals that are of high quality and equally high potential, you'll set up a potential referral machine.

There are "referral clubs," and many service organizations, such as Rotary, encourage members to do this. I still work with a graphics designer that my printer recommended, and I still work with that printer—20 years later.

But I'm talking about finding those relatively few people who can legitimately provide reciprocity and sending them as much business as you can. That's the most efficacious "thank-you" note of all—and these gestures are fondly remembered for years.

For your more traditional clients who provide referrals, send two items:

- A nice, handwritten, hard-copy thank-you note.
- A periodic update of your work with the referral. (That will remind the referral source to provide more, in the win/win/win tradition.)

You can also provide advice and ideas. For example, I found that one client who was excellent at referring me had a daughter who was thinking of attending a school that my daughter had also considered. I brought in the literature for him and offered my daughter's number for his daughter if she wanted to compare notes. On another occasion, I gave a ski-buff client advice on a slope I had visited: the best routes, accommodations, and so on.

In a grayer area, I've found it effective to help referral sources to get into clubs or find tickets for certain events. In other words, I've acted as a sponsor and provided "hot lines" for bargains and priority treatment. So long as I'm not providing a direct financial benefit, but attesting to character or providing a third-party reference, I've always found that safe and appropriate.

In summary, you can reward independent referral sources with referral fees under certain conditions; you can provide advice and gratitude to anyone under any conditions. And you can reciprocate with your own referrals to anyone you choose, which will create a solid and long-lived bond.

Further, keep your referral sources informed of your progress (short of disclosing any confidential information, of course). This helps to

- Demonstrate your ongoing appreciation.
- Keep them apprised of how much they did to create a win/win/win dynamic.
- Keep your name and results in front of them to engender further referrals.

Let's turn now to how you institutionalize yourself in your current and future clients.

CHAPTER 5

INSTITUTIONALIZING YOUR PRESENCE

HOW DOGS SET THE STANDARD FOR BEING INVITED IN AND NEVER LEAVING

JOINING INTERNAL GROUPS

When I worked with Calgon years ago, its field force was far more expert in engineering than in selling. Its representatives were experts in water management, effluent cleaning, environmental concerns, and so on. Some had engineering backgrounds, some chemical, and some mechanical.

When they spoke to technical people, they were speaking a common language. But they didn't do as well when they were competing with pure marketing professionals from the competition, who were often dealing with the people making buying decisions.

The resolution to this disparity was to insert Calgon people into internal client management and implementation teams. For example, a seven-person client task force on improving service to one of the firm's customers might be made up of an account manager, four engineers, a compliance expert, *and the Calgon representative*. In wide-ranging clients dealing with diverse issues, Calgon field engineers became members of internal groups. Once they began making substantive contributions and forming collegial relationships, *they were almost impossible to replace.* (In fact, one of the issues for Calgon was ensuring that the same person remained with that account, and turnover became an even more crucial account retention issue.)

We were all amazed at the success of this approach, the client reception, and the much greater comfort and effectiveness of the Calgon engineers, who were now more persuasive than ever in their own element. It was like asking a video-obsessed teenager to become a technical advisor for "Mortal Combat" or "Angry Birds."

A high-quality marriage made in heaven.

I learned this lesson. Later, at Hewlett-Packard, which used scores of external consultants, from solo practitioners to huge firms, it became apparent that the firm liked an "intimate" relationship with consultants, since the HP people were highly innovative and creative in attacking their challenges. I volunteered to have an internal voice mail system (apart from my own office's system), have access to HP's intranet, and attend virtual meetings no matter where I was in the world.

That made the difference, and I became an advisor to my own interests. Not only did I create close relationships with my current decision makers and referral sources, but I was working alongside HP "up-and-comers," high-potential talent that eventually partnered with me at higher levels and provided still more potent referrals.

Actors talk about "breaking the fourth wall" when they address the audience and puncture their role in the perform-

---

Listen Up!

Referrals are more frequent and of higher quality when they are provided for close friends and colleagues.

ance. Similarly, we break that artificial wall when we partner with the client *not as outsiders, but as insiders.*

What kind of internal efforts are being made that you can participate in? Here are some possibilities:

- Task forces on short-term assignment to deal with crises
- Standing committees for long-term improvement, such as improving client retention
- Client support teams seeking to implement and complete key projects
- Quality and review committees seeking to improve operations and create best practices
- Training and development programs to improve expertise and skills
- R&D teams to improve the competitive nature of products and services

Referrals are most effective when they aren't given as a special event (we've talked earlier about building them into your conversations and process), but rather are an ongoing aspect of your relationship. When you're partnering internally, these suggestions emerge very naturally; for example:

"Good to see you today. Before we start, I wanted to mention that I was talking to my counterpart at Acme, Inc., yesterday and mentioned your work for us. Here's his contact information; he's expecting your call."

Or

"Do me a favor and contact this woman over in European operations. She has the same problem we had

last year when you began working with our committee, and I think you can save her a ton of time and
money. She's on the fourth floor, and I know she's
here today."

In these cases, it's important that you drop everything you're
doing at that instant and engage in the following discipline:

1. Thank your current contact.

2. Carefully take the name and ask for even more
   particulars ("Do you have her cell phone number, as
   well?").

3. Write in your calendar your short-term action plan,
   for example, heading for the fourth floor when you're
   done here or calling someone during a break in the
   meeting.

4. Create the new contact and then get back to your
   referral source with progress and an update.

Internal groups can also be informal. The alternatives
given earlier are defined by regular meetings, agendas, a roster
of members, clear objectives (usually!), and a "purpose." However, there are informal groups that are equally valuable.

Here are a few I've found to be great sources of consultant "integration" and internal acceptance:

- Participate in organizational fund drives and
  charitable events. Since the proceeds go to nonprofit
  third parties, there is no conflict here, and your
  contributions will be well received.

- Offer to serve on ad hoc committees formed to
  decorate for a holiday, celebrate someone's
  anniversary, and so forth.

- If there are softball, foosball, or other competitive events, see if you can join a team when you're around.
- Don't eat in the executive dining room (at least, not all the time). Use the cafeteria and dine with people who accept you as one of the regulars.
- Come early and stay late on occasion. There's nothing wrong with having coffee (bring the doughnuts yourself on occasion), a working lunch at someone's desk, or a drink after a late night at the office.

Formally or informally, when you join internal groups, you become more "one of the gang" and not so much a vendor, supplier, outsider, or consultant. Of course, you'll have to observe the protocols and expectations—you can't learn something over lunch and run to tell your buyer about it! And you can't tell your colleagues over coffee something you learned in the buyer's office.

However, most buyers are very supportive of consultants integrating into the culture and zeitgeist of the organization. You'll find that this is also a powerful way to gain frequent and productive referrals.

PROVIDING EXTRA VALUE (WITHOUT LOSING YOUR SHIRT)

Scope creep. The client asks you to do additional work and provide additional value without additional compensation. This is usually nonmalicious, with the client simply believing you can do something additional "while you're there." It's enabled by consultants who fear ever saying no.

Scope seep. The consultant unilaterally provides extra help and
value beyond the project scope on the superficial basis
that it's easy and he owes the client that much and the
underlying basis of very poor self-esteem and an
attempt to justify one's fee with additional work. This
may not even stop at washing the windows and
sweeping the floor. (I once heard a professional speaker
say, "I'm just a hired hand when I'm on the client site."
Try telling that to your doctor or your lawyer when you
engage her.)

Underpromise and overdeliver. This is a bromide that's so
vacuous and inane that one scarcely knows where to
begin with it, since it suggests a belief system of
inequality and subservience rather than of partnership
and peer-level relationships.

You can provide extra value without falling into any of
these traps. That extra value endears you to the buyer and
prompts repeat and referral business.

As presented in the following case study, I didn't take any
actions other than to observe what was going on, validate what
I thought was happening, and chat with my buyer. My buyer
asked if I could help, not if I'd help for free. And I drew up a
proposal covering my three points that was readily accepted that
week and resulted in $55,000 on top of my six-figure retainer.

Listen Up!
*Providing value is about acting as an advisor, not
necessarily as a pair of hands. It's your brain that's
important.*

The president could have decided to handle all of this
himself or through his own people, and I still would have gar-

CASE STUDY: Miss March

While working with Calgon on retainer, I was on site and roaming around the operation to familiarize myself with the terms, procedures, and processes that I'd hear about in meetings. My wanderings took me to a warehouse across town that even the senior management never visited. It held chemicals for delivery to clients.

As I walked around (I had a company pass), I found a very conspicuous "pinup" calendar on a wall, something I hadn't seen for a decade. It said, "Miss March."

"What is that?" I asked a worker nearby.

"Miss March," he accurately replied.

I ambled into the supervisor's small office and said, "What is that calendar out there?"

"Miss March," he verified.

"Are you aware that the calendar can be construed to represent a hostile workplace environment, is against company policy, and can easily lead to a lawsuit?"

"Come on, this is a warehouse, and that's just Miss March."

At the end of the day, I met with the president as planned. After our agenda was completed, I related my warehouse experience. He was outraged, and he began to reach for the phone.

"You actually have three issues," I noted.

"What do you mean?"

"First, the calendar has to come down, as does anything similar we don't know about. I'm wondering how many people in management may have seen that, by the way. Second, you clearly need an education or reeducation about laws, ethics, and policy. Third, your human resources department is obviously asleep at the switch. It's not monitoring the environment."

"Can you help us with all of that?"

"Sure; let me put something in writing for you."

nered the credit for providing the insights and impetus. He could even have hired another consultant—a specialist in sexual harassment, for example—and the credit for that action still would have been mine.

It's nice to make money from the added value, but it's not a prerequisite or criterion for creating such value. You have a trusted role with your buyer (and others), and you can leverage that role to provide advice, counsel, observations, ideas, and so forth. Just remember to adhere to the "what," not the "how," until such time as you're asked to actually present a proposal and tackle the challenges.

Somewhere about 10,000 years ago, wild wolves were first domesticated when it turned out that those hanging out around human campsites actually provided value in return for being thrown food scraps. That value included garbage disposal, warnings of danger, protection against enemies and predators, and amusement. These wolves became dogs, one of the most impressive species evolutions in history. No other species has ever been domesticated to the extent that dogs have and to fulfill the varied roles that dogs occupy.

They were invited in, and now we can't get them out!

By that I mean, most household canine pets do absolutely nothing in the way of providing value other than the standard unqualified love and affection. They no longer herd, they don't hunt, they rarely protect (most are ill equipped to do so), and they can't help with the house. On the other hand, we feed them, protect them, provide health care, provide housing, groom them, and otherwise coddle them. Dogs sleep on the bed, eat table scraps, and have more health checkups than most humans.

Now, I'm a dog person and I'm as guilty as anyone, although I like to think our German shepherd offers some semblance of backup security. (Interestingly, he and our beagle use the house and ground alarm systems to tell them someone is out there, not their own senses any more, which makes them about as responsive as I am.) But there you have it.

The same principle holds with consultants. As one CEO introduced me (he had worked with me before elsewhere):

"Like any good consultant, Alan will ingratiate himself into our systems and be nearly impossible to remove." There was nervous laughter, including my own.

The more value you provide while looking out for your own interests, the more likely it is that you'll not only never be asked to leave, but be asked to do more and more. "Alan knows so much about us and understands us so well, why not give him that project instead of hiring another outsider?" You'll also be the primary beneficiary of anyone asking about help, or how to replicate your client's success, or for a recommendation.

I wouldn't advise unqualified affection or trying for scraps in the executive dining room, but I would advise that you take on more issues than your current project calls for, make more observations than your current needs would dictate, and reach some conclusions that your client will truly value.

That's symbiosis.

CREATING LATERAL CONTACTS

Lateral contacts are those at the same level at which you're currently dealing. Some examples:

- Your current buyer's peers in the company hierarchy
- Your buyer's peers at vendors and suppliers
- Your buyer's peers in social clubs
- Your buyer's peers in professional associations
- Your buyer's peers in customers
- A professional provider's peers (e.g., your accountant)
- A social acquaintance's peers
- A family member's peers

The reason I'm dealing with these relationships in this separate discussion is that peer-to-peer referrals are the most powerful. Subordinate-to-superior referrals don't have the same power because of perceived differences in perspective, and superior-to-subordinate referrals usually mean you're being delegated to a non-buyer and generally dismissed. While there are exceptions, peer-to-peer discussions about you are the platinum standard.

Listen Up!
The best way to get people to talk about you to their peers is to make them look smart, prescient, and successful.

We've also been speaking about techniques to stimulate these referrals, to use the most effective language to encourage them, and to be assertive in pursuing them. Let's discuss here how they occur "spontaneously," without your direct intervention.

Why do you mention and promote others' services to third parties? If you consider what prompts you to do so, you'll understand what dynamics you should strive to create so that others will do this for you. Let me suggest the keys to spontaneous referrals that I've experienced, and that should match your own experiences:

- *Excellent responsiveness.* People are blown away by service providers who either are readily accessible or respond to inquiries quickly. My own service standard is to return all phone calls within 90 minutes during business hours, and all e-mail within a day (and it's usually within a few hours).

- *Meeting or beating deadlines.* Make sure you have what you need on time or well before it's needed, so that there's never a need to follow up in a panic.

- *Doing great work.* Perfection isn't the aim, but success is. Your work should be outstanding and should meet or surpass the client's objectives on a consistent basis.
- *Intelligent handling of errors.* You should admit to mistakes and correct them. Leave defensiveness and ego at the door. Share credit, but personally accept blame.
- *Make the client the star.* Create deliverables and results that shine on the client's judgment and planning.
- *Have respect.* Have respect for the individual who needs assistance and accept the collegial (and even ethical) obligation to provide the best possible resources for his or her needs.
- *Reciprocity.* Have the belief, explicit or implicit, that the behavior will rebound to help you at some later date through reciprocity or other means.

If these motivators are present for you when you are referring others, then you can create a plan to provide them for your referral sources. To what degree are you serving, behaving, acting, and prompting along these lines? It's always amazed me that people who are consistently late or who make promises that they can't keep are stunned when they rarely receive spontaneous referrals. Who would want to inflict that experience on a third party?!

This extends to your presence and behavior in other aspects of your life and relationships:

- If you are estranged from family members, or if you are sarcastic or less than humble in your attitude toward them, they are unlikely to bother to ever refer anyone to you.

- If you serve on a civic committee or board and you attempt to overwhelm others and refuse to compromise, those other members will not feel the urge to recommend you to their business colleagues.
- If you participate in an election to support a candidate, and you are aggressive and hostile toward your opponents' views, you will make permanent enemies in the community.
- If you are rude or nonparticipative at your social club, you will be alienating a prime source of spontaneous referrals.
- If you do not participate and never offer assistance in your trade and professional associations, other members won't even know enough about you to recommend you to others.

I could go on and on in a 360-degree arc. Every day, you have the ability to prompt spontaneous referrals, but, at best, you may be doing nothing to encourage them, and, at worst, you may be discouraging them.

I'm not suggesting that you curtail your right to free speech or tolerate people whom you don't care to associate with, but I am suggesting that you look around at those who are best at obtaining referral business: Realtors, insurance sales-people, car dealers, attorneys, designers, and so forth. Ask yourself how they do it, often within narrower communities than your own.

You'll find that they are adept at encouraging peers, colleagues, and the "lateral" level of communications to mention them. For example, are you

- Mentoring or coaching others in your profession, in your hobbies, or in your other interests?

- Writing newspaper articles, columns, or letters to the editor that help to establish both your expertise and your constructive ideas?
- Contributing to your professional associations with presentations, interviews, articles, new member drives, and/or financial support?

SHARING OWNERSHIP OF INTELLECTUAL PROPERTY

Consult your attorney, but in general, as discussed through this book,

- The intellectual property that you bring to a client, you also take away again. What you own, you keep.
- The intellectual property of the client remains that of the client, so you cannot take that away and use it independently.
- Anything you create together, you both own, subject to any agreements, protocols, and discussions that you have. You may both use it on other occasions, barring the use of confidential material; or you may agree that only one or the other may use it for other purposes; or its use may be restricted to solely the purposes for which it was jointly created by you and the client.

What I want to discuss here is how to share intellectual property to institutionalize your presence within a client. Think of your IP as the wolf who comes to dinner and is domesticated and retained by the client.

By "sharing intellectual property" I mean providing it for the client, for equitable compensation, and with the intent that it be used on an ongoing basis in lieu of your presence.

CASE STUDY: The Rocket Ship

At a meeting at Hewlett-Packard, I had cut a Gordian knot of conflicting views on a new project by suggesting that what was actually needed was "escape velocity": the ability to launch this initiative despite the "gravity" of deeply held beliefs, routine behaviors, and conflicting interests.

I drew a rudimentary rocket ship and rules for achieving escape velocity with new projects. I thought it went well, and that was the end of it.

However, returning a month later, I found my drawing and rules pinned up in a high-traffic area where everyone could keep referring to them. I decided that it would make sense to provide something more formal and easier for the client to disseminate, with my blessing. That rocket ship and its launch rules created great visibility, credibility, and referrals within HP, even though I was a six-hour plane ride away most of the time.

The intellectual property may be far more sophisticated than my rocket ship and, unlike my extemporaneous example, far more precedented. For example, you may have a proprietary approach to integrating IT capabilities into strategy formulation, using them as a determinant of direction and not merely an implementer of direction. You might have used this approach with a succession of clients, used it in public workshops, provided manuals and instructions for adopting the process, and so forth.

Suppose you suggest to your client, Acme, that it be extended rights to use the approach internally, in domestic and foreign subsidiaries, customized to its particular content and audience by you, with instructors and facilitators prepared by you. Acme would not require your presence to use this annually at strategy reviews, although you would be available should there be technical questions. You would even allow Acme to call this

"The Acme Technical Strategy Integration." It may differ from your generic model by 15 or 20 percent. The new version has a shared copyright, held by you and Acme. Acme is not permitted to use the approach with vendors or customers, but only within its own organization for a period agreed upon by both parties.

Voilà, that is shared ownership.

Listen Up!
If you have a trusting relationship, you don't have to worry about theft or broken agreements. Partners don't cheat each other.

I think you can imagine just how much referral business is accelerated when joint intellectual property is making the rounds of a large organization, especially if it becomes the default intervention for many issues. Buyers will invite you in to explain, install, and monitor the use of the technologies; outsiders (especially vendors seeking preferred status) will want to emulate their client. (This is why the agreement is always for use within the client solely, and not with others.)

Here are some conditions to determine when and if to share your intellectual property with a client, beyond your own personal application:

- What IP do you possess that is most amenable to others learning and delivering it without your being present?
- Can you devise an easy and rapid training program for implementers and/or facilitators? (For example, can they work with you on your personal implementation?)
- Does the client have ample opportunity to apply it on a repetitive and widespread basis?

- Is it a "good deal" for both parties, with the client paying less than would be required for you to do it all, but you receiving equitable compensation for much less labor intensity?
- What is the proper duration? Is it for a year, or renewable annually, or for several years, or in perpetuity? (Your fees increase accordingly.)
- What is the channel for referrals as the system is utilized and others become interested?
- How is the client updated as you update your IP and continue to improve it?

These are pleasant problems and constructive issues. Sharing ownership of IP can revitalize assets that you already own, but that are older or underutilized, increase your "remote" value to the client, decrease labor intensity, and generate ongoing referrals, literally while you sleep. Generally, the larger the client and the higher-ranking the economic buyer, the more likely it is to create these scenarios. But if you think about lateral buyers, which we've discussed earlier in this chapter, you can see how that approach coupled with this concept can be powerful.

DEMONSTRATING UNIQUE VALUE (SOLE SOURCE SOUL)

Unique has become a word that's not so unique anymore. We hear about unique opportunities, people, cars, pets, vacations, and storms. However, unique means "existing as a sole example with no equal."

This is why philosophies that espouse a "unique selling proposition" are non-uniquely silly. Not only won't you create one, but you don't need one. You have to be very, very good, but not "a sole example with no equal," no matter what your life coach or your mother has told you!

So why am I using the word in this segment? Because the relationship that *you* have with *your* buyer in the client organization is unique. Therefore, the value you can bring to that relationship is unique, which is why it is so difficult to displace a consultant who has a trusting relationship with a buyer. The value perceptions are unique, and an outsider—a new consultant—would need dynamite to displace that bond.

I've called this phenomenon "sole source soul." In the (largely governmental) world of requests for proposals (RFPs), there is a technique to avoid the competitive bidding process if you're considered a "sole source": you have a commercially published book, distinctive intellectual property, specialized models, relevant travel, or work in various environments that merit hiring you outside of normal bidding. This is justified because you are the "sole source" for that client's needs. (Sometimes, sympathetic buyers will actually create RFPs that only you can fill along these same lines; for example, we need someone living in Edina who has traveled extensively in Canada and Mexico and has experience teaching graduate-level courses in Spanish and English.)

I'm suggesting here that referrals—especially spontaneous referrals, without your prompting for them—will be accelerated when you are providing unique value on an ongoing basis.

Listen Up!

Look around. Ask yourself why things look the way they do, why people are acting the way they do, and why change is readily accepted or difficult to implement. Don't simply wear the blinders of your project.

So how do we create such continual unique value for clients? Here are techniques that I've gleaned from my own quarter-century of consulting and my global mentoring communities.

Alan's Ongoing Value Sources

1. Look around the environment, and don't assume something is beyond your purview or is irrelevant. (Think of the warehouse case study earlier in this chapter.) This is neither scope creep nor scope seep. Bring to your buyer's attention incongruities, contradictions, and dangers in the environment.

    Example: The client's signage outside is being blocked by untrimmed bushes, or one elevator constantly leaves a four-inch gap and isn't flush with the landing.

2. Suggest things that will make the client's day easier. Why is the buyer rushing around, coming in early, staying late, disorganized, out of touch, or whatever? Has the buyer merely become adept at adjusting to bad habits rather than creating better ones?

    Example: Ask the buyer why his presence was required at a meeting where information was merely exchanged among participants and decisions or policy reviews weren't required.

3. Think about where most of the energy is going. Are people usually talking about the client, the product, and the service? Or are they talking about their lack of resources, their desire for a better office, or their unhappiness with a recent evaluation? How much productivity is being lost to internal turf conflicts and personal dissatisfaction?

Example: Suggest that a "hotline" or ombudsman be created to deal with anonymous employee concerns and suggestions.

4. Look for ways to improve responsiveness. Is your client taking too long to respond to her customers? Are there backlogs of requests, mail, voice mail, e-mails, and general inquiries? Is there even a service standard for timeliness of response? (Good restaurants generally require that patrons be greeted and asked about having drinks within two minutes of being seated.)

Example: Can the client create a "triage" of critical, important, and mundane requests, with different response times for each? Can more responses be automated and/or customer-controlled? (Amtrak uses an extensive and sophisticated automated voice system to attend to many reservation requests and has extended its online capability to include reservation changes during a trip.)

5. Think about whether the structure makes sense. The majority of leaders I've worked with have *too large* a span of control. This may be because of a lack of trust, a belief that direct reports equal importance, or simply the inertia of an ancient command structure. Can you recommend that the client consider a leaner and more direct hierarchy?

Example: One of my clients placed his human resources vice president concurrently in charge of the Mexican operation, with the rationale that the two jobs could easily be filled by one person, and the HR dimension would receive far more credibility from the direct involvement of a line operation.

I want to strongly reemphasize that you should not take this on as your project or as part of an existing project, or even recommend it as a new project, although the last condition might happen in certain circumstances, as in the warehouse example. The point is that you can raise issues *that the client can usually deal with unilaterally.* There is no specialized skill, merely the observation that simple changes can yield huge results.

If you consider yourself a partner of the buyer, then this behavior makes immediate sense, since this is how partners treat each other—they suggest improvements and point out potential problems. The more you do this casually, during normal conversations about your project, the more the client will come to rely on you, appreciate your insights, and trust your judgment. Those dynamics stimulate referrals.

I've said throughout the book to this point that you should think not in terms of an event, but of a process. Similarly, you should think in terms of a partner, not a client. And you should think in terms of creating reliance, not simply a transaction.

How have you reacted to people who have casually mentioned to you some suggestions that were immediately useful and important? You've thanked them, looked forward to seeing them again, and been ready to recommend them to anyone who needed such value.

MY GREATEST REFERRAL

I ASKED SOME COLLEAGUES in my Mentor Program and other communities to provide examples of their "greatest referral." I thought you'd profit from the variety and the sources.

Kelli Richards
President & CEO
The All Access Group, LLC
www.allaccessgroup.com

As a veteran consultant, mentor, producer, and coach, referrals from both colleagues and satisfied clients are the lifeblood of my business. I could share many examples, but probably one of the most rewarding new pieces of business was when my co-producer and I were hired by the United Nations to produce a fund-raiser event in Los Angeles to clear land mines. The artists performing at this event were none other than Sir Paul McCartney, Brian Wilson (Beach Boys), and Stephen Stills (Crosby Stills & Nash). Oh, and it was hosted by Jay Leno.

It was our job to manage the talent and to ensure that the evening ran smoothly; it was a big success and a truly magical evening to witness. Participating in an event of this stature was a real high point in the production side of my career to that point, though I'd been a producer for many years by then. My co-producer (Steve Macfadyen) and I were referred to the U.N. by one of our longtime colleagues, Michael Jensen, one of the most revered publicists in music today. I suppose one could argue that luck played a role in our securing this opportunity, but I prefer to acknowledge the power of credible referrals as the result of earned stature and long-term trusted relationships.

My advice to others seeking referrals (of any kind) is, first and foremost, to pay attention to the care and feeding of the long-term relationships in your network; nurture them and keep them strong and healthy. That's where the bulk of your referrals will most likely come from. And also, don't hesitate to reach out and make requests of people in your network when you want or need a specific referral from someone. This is "The Aladdin Factor" at work. Generally people are happy to support you if they know, like, and trust you—and if you have something of real value to offer that will reflect well on the person creating the referral. It's all about give and take.

Amanda Setili
Managing Partner
Setili & Associates, LLC
Atlanta, Georgia

My greatest referral was provided by a new prospect, on the first day that I had ever met him. The person he referred me to, a vice president with a Fortune 500 consumer services company, engaged my firm for a consulting project after only one or two meetings.

The experience taught me to ask for referrals much earlier in a relationship, which has helped me grow my business faster. And, the project that resulted from the referral was high value, fun, and right in my sweet spot.

Here are some factors that helped to make this a great referral.

First, I met the referral source through an introduction from one of my favorite clients, someone whom I've done high-value work with, who really "gets" what I do, and who understands how I'm differentiated from other consultants. I've learned that anyone he introduces me to will be a great fit and a pleasure to work with.

Second, I demonstrated my capability and provided value to the referral source in our initial meeting. I listened carefully when he shared the strategic challenges his company was facing, and did my best to help him think through some of these issues as we spoke that day. I find that by asking good questions, by helping a prospect break his problems down into pieces, and by framing the issues, I can be of great value, even in the course of just one meeting. Toward the end of the meeting—and bear in mind, this was the first time I had ever met him—I asked him whom he would be willing to refer me to.

Third, I prompted him for names. After saying he'd be happy to refer me, he had trouble coming up with specific names. When he said, "I'd love to; I'll think about it and get back to you," I knew I was unlikely to hear back, despite his sincere intention to help. He was busy, and had other priorities. As a thought starter, I said, "What about someone you worked with at your prior company, or at one of the not-for-profit boards you've served on?" Just this small nudge helped him think of exactly the right person to refer me to.

Fourth, I asked him to share some insight on the person's background, and how I might be able to help them as a consultant. Through this exploration process, I identified several things that the person and I had in common, and was primed for a great entry.

And finally, I reported back to him several times on the success of the project that he had helped me secure, and how much I appreciated his introducing me. I made a point of staying in touch, visiting him when he had time, and connecting him to others that he would benefit from knowing. He's become a good friend.

Tim Forrest
Tim Forrest Consulting
St. Simons Island, Georgia
www.timforrest.com

My greatest referral resulted in more than a decade of business, millions in sales, and trips to the beautiful Caribbean with an apartment overlooking the beach, and I gained a friend in the process.

It all started with a simple comment, "Tim, a friend is in the process of planning a new food enterprise in the Caribbean and needs help. Why don't you call him?"

I was excited for many reasons regarding this conversation with Jim. He was then controller at a Borden facility, and we were improving the business from losing more than a quarter of a million dollars per month to finally making money.

Jim provided the initial phone introductions and gave me the contact information for Joe Melendez. It turned out that Joe and I had worked for the same company years before and hit it off immediately. We talked about his ideas and opportunity, and he provided me full access to his situation and needs. We were able to achieve many things working together, including landing the Kmart snack bar business and Chili's Restaurant contract.

Trust was the main ingredient in gaining this referral. Jim trusted that I might assist his friend in the Caribbean. Joe also had a feeling of trust that my involvement would somehow help his business prosper. These feelings of trust paved the way of our relationship and the exchange of information back and forth that resulted in success that did not come for several months after the initial introductions.

In this ongoing exchange of information, we were able to find value in my offerings, and after a period of many months shipped the first container of product to his food company. That first cargo container turned into another and then another as we grew the business together. The millions in business did not occur overnight, and we had many issues to battle and resolve together. Fortunately, the trust and our relationship stayed intact as we worked to provide service to the Caribbean food enterprise and only my second client in my then very young company.

The most important component to gaining and then growing this piece of referral business was the trust and ongoing relationship with all the contacts involved. The trust opened the door for Jim to refer me to his friend in the Caribbean. And the trust of Joe allowed me to demonstrate and add value to his food enterprise with new products and methods of doing business.

Develop relationships of trust and bring value to interested parties. This is the basis of great referral business, and everyone has the ability to develop these basic skills if they so choose. It might seem too simple a formula, but trust builds the path to success.

Rabbi Issamar Ginzberg
Monetized Intellect Consulting
Brooklyn, New York

I have a client, a Mr. T., whom I met when I sent him a message via Facebook thanking him for some helpful educational material for students that he had available for download on his site.

After getting my Facebook private message (which was not sent in any attempt to generate business at all), T. responded saying that he thanked me for my kind words . . . and that he had researched my work online and that he would be interested in hiring me to help him with his business. I was grateful for this person's work (which was why I originally contacted him), and knowing his budget was limited, gave him a break on the cost of the project.

Since that time, I have not had much interaction with T.—but every so often I get a call or an e-mail from someone whom he has recommended me to, with a request to set up a meeting, mainly from nonprofits and public speakers.

One of those calls came from a very prominent speaker and consultant who has since hired me to add new streams of revenue to his business, and deleverage the business from being attached to his personal speaking engagements and from "time for dollars" to a value-based proposition.

When this client met me the first time (I know this sounds unbelievable!), we had a discussion, and the client took careful notes of everything I said on a BlackBerry PDA, and at the close of the consultation startled me with the following request: "Please take your sketches and diagrams away with you, as not a soul is allowed to know that I have hired you. I have many close friends that are consultants, and they would be very offended that I chose you above them, which is why I took notes on my BlackBerry, so not a trace of your visit remains."

Since that time, that person has been involved in getting me new business, speaking opportunities, and connections in different countries, and, in truth, also gave me much more confidence in my ability to help people that "already know it all." I'm consulting people old enough to be my grandma!

In a second speech I gave, I spoke to an association of language translation specialists, about which someone told me, "For the amount they paid you, you shouldn't even be getting out of bed!" and someone who attended that speech put in a recommendation for me with Google to go speak at Google Israel (still working on the details on that one!). So, you truly never know where your referrals and best business will come from . . .

Andrew Miller
President, ACM Consulting Inc.
Toronto, Ontario
Canada

My greatest referral came from the senior vice president of a midsized hospital. I had done a great deal of volunteer work to help develop one of the young leadership groups in the hospital and had worked directly with this senior VP in a volunteer capacity. Through this volunteer work, we developed a strong relationship and realized we had very similar views on how to improve leadership and operations in a health-care environment. I was also helping him better understand some of the new government policies that were being implemented to govern the purchasing of goods and services by public-sector organizations.

He eventually became a client for a small project focused on making better buying decisions for the organization. Once the project was completed, I asked him for referrals to three other organizations, and he gave me a list of names of people who were executives and decision makers at 11 other hospitals. He told me to use his name, and we drafted a correspondence to them stating the value that was achieved from our project and that they should take the time out to meet with me.

That referral came about 15 months ago. Since then, I have contacted all 11 organizations and had meetings with almost all of them. Many of them would never have seen me without his endorsement, as he is thought of very highly in the industry. Three of the organizations have since become my clients, and this has led to other referrals and other clients.

The original list of names has led to well over six figures worth of business for me over the last 15 months, with some of the relationships still being developed and may lead to future business. One executive has left her original organization, and her new organization has become my client. The senior VP himself has now moved organizations and has become president and CEO of a different hospital, and we are planning on doing additional work together to bring value to his new organization. The initial list of people continues to provide value as I meet and work with different organizations and executives who leave their companies for new organizations.

At the outset, I knew that he would be happy to provide me with a referral, but I did not know the impact that one referral source would have on my business. Keeping the relationship strong and continuing to provide him with tremendous value are things that I continue to focus on. I also want to continue to make him look good for providing the referrals by delivering tremendous value to my clients. You never know where the next great referral will come from, so don't be afraid to ask!

Gail S. Bower, President
Bower & Co. Consulting LLC

My greatest referral changed the course of my life.

I worked in advertising and PR at an ad agency in Philadelphia and negotiated the sponsorship by my PR client of an important citywide event. At the time, I was planning to leave the agency and go out on my own. The event producer, also independent, was very supportive of this decision and briefly became a mentor to me, though we never met in person.

It was 1987, the year marking the bicentennial of the U.S. Constitution, written in Philadelphia. I assumed the tourism organization here would need assistance marketing the celebration. My mentor introduced me to the tourism leaders, who, I learned, actually were not responsible for the bicentennial but had other projects in mind for me. They had just launched a series of music festivals designed to drive tourism; they brought me in as an independent event producer and marketer to support their efforts.

This affiliation led to a 20-year alliance with another collaborator of the tourism organization, one of the most influential producers of music festivals in the world. Through this company, I produced, marketed, developed revenue sources, and/or operated festivals such as the Newport Jazz Festival, Newport Folk Festival, Essence Music Festival, New Orleans Jazz & Heritage Festival, and the largest free public events that were part of both of former President Clinton's inaugurations.

The experiences I gained through these festivals would also contribute to the rich intellectual capital that consulting clients 25 years later would find so valuable.

A couple of years ago, I finally met my early mentor in person. She was astonished to learn the impact that her single referral had on my life and career.

Steven B. Levy
Lexician Consulting

My greatest referral, oddly enough, led to a potential consulting engagement that I was unable to land. In other words, from this referral, I got $0.00. At least, that's what I earned directly.

But I also got a business from it, a successful consulting business.

About two years ago, I left my senior leadership position at a Fortune 50 corporation, burned out but not really ready to retire. I wasn't sure what to do next, but I figured my decades of leadership experience, project-management successes, and hard-won business smarts could provide advice and direction to any number of companies—in essence, the consultant role.

I'd renewed contact with a number of people I'd met during my corporate sojourn; they knew I was looking to do more than hang out at my vacation home and tune up my golf game. (Perhaps, too, they'd seen me play and realized other golfers might live longer if I stayed off the course.) One day, a contact called me and said, "I have a customer looking into this new legal project management concept. I know you've been pushing this approach to handling legal work for years, so I suggested they call you."

I thanked him and hung up the phone, and within a minute it rang again. It was his customer, calling to ask me about training them in legal project management. I was totally unprepared, and I know it showed. I also knew they were looking to hire a big firm, and I wasn't at the time aware of how to compete with big consulting firms. In any case, I had little hope of winning that engagement at that time, but I had a very interesting conversation for 30 or 40 minutes.

As I made some notes when the call ended, I began thinking of things I should have said—not to win that piece of business, but to define legal project management itself. The caller had only the vaguest idea of what it could or should be, but they had a sense that it could help them become more efficient. I recognized that I had stumbled across a particular field that truly leveraged so much of what I'd learned during 35 years in the business world: managing projects, helping attorneys succeed, building efficiency, leading people who don't take well to traditional management styles, applying the principles of economics to the practice of law. In effect, I had an opportunity to create a new field just as it was starting to gain the first trickle of momentum.

I got my consulting act together, developed a clear message and vision, and began pitching clients. I took every opportunity to speak about legal project management. Most important, I wrote the first book on the subject, a book that has garnered outstanding reviews, both in print and via word of mouth, and that has become the standard work on the subject. And my consulting business has started to blossom. I'm not only doing the right thing at the right time, but it's something I'm passionately committed to, something that meshes perfectly with my collected experience.

And it all came from a referral for an engagement that I didn't win.

Shawn Casemore
President
Casemore and Co.

While preparing to launch my consulting practice, I, like many others, read *Million Dollar Consulting* and began to follow Alan Weiss. After much consideration, I joined Alan's mentor program to expand my knowledge in the field of consulting. It did not take much time to select my mentor, Phil Symchych, who was a fellow Canadian, had a proven track record as a very successful consultant, and had a reputation for helping business owners dramatically improve and grow their businesses.

I was contacted one day out of the blue by Phil, who asked if I would be interested in assisting one of his clients. This client was considering making a capital investment in a CNC machine. I was somewhat surprised by Phil's generosity at introducing me to his client, and, more important, recommending the value I could deliver.

After some brief discussions with Phil, he sent an e-mail to his client, introducing me. Shortly thereafter I received a phone call, and following a brief discussion, we agreed on the objectives, measures, and value of proceeding with the relationship. I was amazed that in one phone call, I was able to move directly into such a conversation without spending considerable time providing credibility or building a relationship. I would like to think the expeditious bond was the result of my ability to build strong relationships. However, it was clear that the relationship Phil had with his client was the underlying reason for their inherent trust in me.

This was my first up-close-and-personal experience with referrals. I realized the sheer power of Phil's referral, and how building relationships with not only potential clients, but also those who assisted clients in the planning for and spending of capital funds would be the best possible source of future business. After months of Phil telling me I needed to build relationships with bankers and accountants, it was as if someone had just turned on the light.

Needless to say, the client engagement went very well. I negotiated substantial savings and favorable terms for my new client, which allowed them to invest less working capital and save their valuable time in the process.

As a result of the referral, I was able to gain a new client for future business, a glowing testimonial, and another referral source for future business. I have listened to Alan say numerous times, "Referrals are the coinage of my realm"; however, this statement never had true meaning until the day that I received my first referral.

Mark F. Weiss
Attorney at Law
Advisory Law Group

I'm a health-care attorney in Los Angeles and Santa Barbara.

Several years ago, I met a corporate attorney at a bar association function. In response to his query about my practice, I told him that instead of focusing on task-oriented projects, such as an individual contract, I work with physician groups and entrepreneurs in health care on a relationship basis, bringing transformational change to their business.

Within a week, he called to refer a new client. That work generated an immediate $20,000 or so in fees, but that's not the real impact of the referral.

Rather, within a month of the initial referral, that first new client referred an extremely entrepreneurial physician who, over the course of the many years I worked with him, paid several million dollars in fees.

Not bad for a five-minute conversation over drinks!

Karen Post
President
Brain Tattoo Branding
Tampa, Florida

In August of 2009, I was invited to follow Alan Weiss on Twitter. As he was one of my most valued coaches, I signed up. That evening, I was reviewing Alan's timeline and stumbled upon a retweet stating that someone was looking for a branding consultant. The post came from another one of Alan's mentees, a manufacturing professional named Alan Fortier. I responded to

Alan Fortier, and, as it turned out, he was assisting one of his clients that needed a branding consultant. I forwarded all of my information, and we scheduled a conference.

While my credentials and experience were sound and relevant, having come from Alan Weiss's network and having been a fellow Alan Weiss mentee, this made my connection to Alan Fortier, the referrer, even stronger.

The client was a global chemical company, and Alan Fortier was tasked with sourcing and screening candidates. After a good amount of dialogue with Alan Fortier, I made the short list of referrals from Alan to the client.

Sixty days later, after submitting a proposal and having a face-to-face meeting, I secured the work that, to date, has turned out to be a high six-figure client.

This was a chain referral that gave me an opportunity to develop an eco brand for a global, public company. I earned a very nice fee, produced some of my best work (from print to social media to broadcast), and learned about an industry that I never really gave much thought to before. This client and project opened up a completely new category of work for me in the industrial sustainability sector. It was not planned, nor did I, at that time, believe Twitter could truly make serious lead referrals. I'm happy to report I was wrong.

Monica Austin Gordon
Gordon Consulting

The wind was fierce in February 2009 as the plane landed. In spite of the severe weather watch, I had a meeting with a member of the Oklahoma National Speakers Association.

Ironically, his name was John Storm, and although we had never met, I was touched by his willingness to meet a novice speaker from California. His philosophy was to "give back" because someone prominent and world-renowned had donated their time to speak at their local chapter.

As John corrected my spelling of the gentleman's name, he strongly recommended I digest anything I could get my hands on written by this master in the industry. Our conversation covered several details, which I struggled to absorb. But two items stuck for sure: John Storm's kindness (he and his wife invited me to an NBA home game that evening), and the name was spelled W-E-I-S-S.

Five weeks later, this referral came into sharper focus as I pulled into the CBS studio parking lot in Los Angeles. This intriguing venue was the stage for the Greater Los Angeles Chapter of NSA's guest speaker, Alan Weiss.

During the interactive workshop, my awe and gratitude spilled over in asking the proverbial novice question, "How much should I charge?" to excitedly shaking Maria Weiss's hand and thanking her for sharing her husband with us.

The dramatic piece of new business that resulted from John's referral was a measurable investment in me. I became my own client. Attending the last Best Practices in Consulting seminar eight months later in Rhode Island led to a day and a half of great information and a personal, uninterrupted 10-minute audience with Alan Weiss. The impact of that meeting and the words that were shared continue to have a profound effect on my life.

Seated on two wide-back chairs facing each other in the hall of the Crowne Plaza Hotel, my internal mantra was: "Be respectful of time; end early. Ask questions for two minutes; listen three times longer; end in eight. Don't gab; shut up and listen . . ."

His sage advice included, "Put the oxygen mask on yourself first, Monica. Don't be afraid, and don't hesitate."

The return on my personal investment continued, as I was one of nine to join Alan for dinner. While riding in his beautiful, custom-made Bentley GTC Speed with two other intriguing guests, I realized I was not reading about possibilities, I was experiencing them. The banter of Phil Symchych and Chad Barr discussing PFMs and BMW driving school were celebrated as I ordered two amazing desserts, presents for me. This referral was exposing me to a world larger than my own backyard, with resources to glean from, opportunities to explore, and relationships to build.

This is my oxygen mask. As I am days away from submitting my first query for consideration, my gratitude is extended to John Storm for pointing me in the right direction and to Alan Weiss for challenging me to gather courage to work on myself. I'm finding the air up here is fine.

Daryl Gerke, Partner
Kimmel Gerke Associates, Ltd.

While not the greatest financial referral, this was kind of fun. Not one, but multiple referrals that had the client clamoring to do business with us. No need to sell this one—the client was so hot to buy he was sizzling.

First, some brief background information. We are electrical engineers who specialize in a very narrow niche, electromagnetic interference and compatibility (EMI/EMC). For the nontechnical, we are "ghostbusters" of the electronics industry.

Our clients often call us when they are in pain. Something is broken, or they have failed a critical test that prevents shipping their product. Expensive either way, and they need help fast. But they do want to make sure whoever they call can solve the problem and not make it worse.

So a typical first step is to ask others for recommendations. This is exactly what our client, a young engineer recently out of school, decided to do. His boss told him to check around, so he first called a favorite college professor to ask if he knew anyone that could help. The first referral: "Call Kimmel Gerke Associates."

Not knowing who we were, he decided to get a second opinion. He called another college professor who had just written an article on EMI/EMC. The second referral: "Call Kimmel Gerke Associates."

The professor also mentioned a nearby EMI/EMC test laboratory. So he decided to call them too. The third referral: "Call Kimmel Gerke Associates."

The next phone call was to us. He said, "Look, I'm a new engineer and I don't know who you are. But every time I call someone, they tell me to call Kimmel Gerke Associates. Either you guys are good, or you have been paying everyone off. Either way, I need help!"

After a brief discussion, it was obvious we could help. So we set up a meeting, reviewed his design, made recommendations, and accompanied him to a test lab to validate the fixes. After the consultation, we knew that if anyone asked him, he would say: "Call Kimmel Gerke Associates!"

The multiple referrals were the result of what Alan Weiss calls "marketing gravity." Thanks to our multiple marketing efforts, the first referral knew us from technical articles we had written. The second referral knew us from our professional society activities. And the third referral knew us from collaborating on several projects.

We've seen this happen a number of times. As engineers, we refer to this as an "exponential multiplier." That is, if one referral doubles your chance of success, a second one quadruples it, and a third one drives it up by a factor of eight. Call it gravity or call it exponential, multiple referrals really work.

Simma Lieberman
President
Simma Lieberman Associates
www.simmalieberman.com

I presented a workshop on life/balance at the Women's Food-service Forum several years ago. I told people to give me their contact information if they wanted to be on my mailing list.

After I returned from the conference, I called those attendees to see how they were using the information from the workshop and offer additional suggestions. I asked those people for the names of anyone else who they thought could benefit from my work. One of the women I spoke with gave me the name of a friend of hers who was a manager at Pillsbury Bakeries and Food Services. We developed a rapport over the phone. She shared some of her training needs with me, and asked if I could help her. Without even meeting me in person, she hired me to design and facilitate a training program on Gender Communications for her employees, along with a facilitator's guide.

We conducted the program in several different locations, and developed a good working relationship.

One of the participants in one of the workshops was a senior leader in human resources. He liked my work and philosophy, and we continued to stay in contact. About a year later, he transferred to an international beverage company owned by the same parent organization as Pillsbury.

The president of the beverage company was a forward thinker. He knew that in order to increase market share, they needed to develop a strategy to increase the diversity of employees at the management level, and that it would take more than simple diversity training. He wanted to find the right consultant who was an expert in diversity to help him.

The HR leader whom I had originally met at Pillsbury referred him to me. After meeting with the president and his team, I was hired to develop and conduct an organizational assessment to use as benchmark and identify their strengths and challenges regarding diversity and all of its dimensions. The work expanded to include facilitation of meetings with the leadership team on benchmarking and best practices, and recruiting and interviewing skills and strategy.

Here was the process:

- Colleague recommended me as a workshop presenter on life/balance for a conference.
- Presented workshop at the conference.
- Asked participants for their cards if they wanted an article from me on the topic.
- Followed up with interested participants.
- Asked for referral.
- Phone call to referral.
- Developed rapport during phone call and was hired to design and facilitate a training program on gender communications.
- Delivered program and developed relationship with an executive participant.
- Maintained contact, and apprised him of the kinds of work I did.
- Executive provided my name to president of large beverage company.
- Representative from beverage company contacted me.
- Met with president of company, which resulted in a six-figure contract.

THE CULT OF CEYK (CALL EVERYONE YOU KNOW)

CAREFUL WHERE YOU STEP; YOU'RE CRUSHING REFERRALS

UNTAPPED REFERRAL SOURCES AROUND YOU

For people who are new to professional services, those who are undergoing a business downturn, and those in need of short-term cash (one of the most difficult positions of all, since this isn't a short-term cash business) I always recommend a fundamental discipline: call everyone you know.

The language you should use is: "I'm calling to let you know the kind of value I'm now providing for my clients with the hope that this might be useful to you or someone you know. If the former, I'd like to have an opportunity to meet with you. If the latter, I'd be appreciative if you could provide an introduction."

One of the problems in a small town is that everyone knows everyone else. I live in Rhode Island, too small to be a real state of the union and more like a state of mind. But the principle is the same: it's hard to hide. If you have a mistress or a lover, it's best to avoid local eyes by meeting them some distance away—

say, Toronto. Similarly, you want to catch yourself before exhibiting undue anger or a rude digit to someone who cuts you off, since it could be the police chief, your bank lending officer, one of your kid's teachers, or your probation officer.

Similarly, if you go around burning bridges in your life, it's going to be very difficult to ferry referrals across the rapids.

You should engage in CEYK at least twice a year. I find that quarterly is not too often if you do it right, with the mindset I've tried to establish with you: I have tremendous value, and I'd be remiss if I didn't present it to as many people as I can, *particularly those I know.*

If you're not careful about where you "step," you may be crushing these fragile referral sources.

You can end your referral journey with these untapped (or too infrequently tapped) sources prematurely by

- Ignoring them.
- Acknowledging them but never using the language given previously.
- Insulting them.
- Creating the impression that they can't help you. (If you brag about doing business only with billion-dollar global firms, which isn't exactly accurate, why should local $100 million firm owners come to you?)
- Being nonresponsive. I seldom provide referrals to anyone who doesn't get back to me to acknowledge them or who never actually bothers to call them.
- Becoming subordinated to a competitor who doesn't make these mistakes and mines the sources far better than you.
- Mismanaging perceptions about yourself and failing to blow your own horn.

- Doing poor work and having people complain about you.

I'm all for freedom of speech, but I have to wonder about shopkeepers who post partisan political signs in their businesses during heated and antagonistic election periods. The signs will seldom sway anyone to vote in any way other than what he intends, but they will sway people to stop patronizing the business of someone who "pokes them in the eye" with competing beliefs when they voluntarily enter the shop.

If you're depending on people to help your business, then stay out of their business!

On the positive side, here's what you should be doing to tap the referral sources all around you. After all, you can never tell when someone who knows someone finds out that what she needs is what you have.

- Volunteer for local charities, fund-raisers, and arts groups.
- Write positive and constructive letters to the editors of local publications. I can't tell you how many people have stopped me to say, "That was a terrific letter; I'm referring others to it."
- Sponsor an event, a ball team, or a performance. My wife and I are sponsoring a ballerina in her twentieth season with the local ballet company.
- Serve on boards and commissions. Use your expertise to help groups that need it, and enable others to see that expertise in action.
- Refer people to others, just as you'd like done to you. Make sure you personally introduce them to get the credit and set the proper expectations of reciprocity.

- Do a favor. Watch a pet during someone's vacation, help to restore a building, give someone a recommendation for school, or provide financial support.
- Provide your home for an event, loan a possession for the theater's props, or find auction items for a fund-raiser.
- Send out press releases about your business, accolades, clients, and so forth to local sources.

Listen Up!

People will form opinions of you in any case. You might as well assertively try to make those opinions positive, on the reasonable expectation that the more positively you're seen, the more likely it is that someone will recommend you to others.

Here are some often-untapped referral sources that are all around you. I'm suggesting that you assiduously and regularly solicit them all for business and referrals. Remember: revenue and referrals are equally important to your business.

Lawyer	Doctor	Accountant	Bookkeeper
Clergy	Designer	Electrician	Plumber
Engineer	Cleaners	Kids' teachers	Shop owners
Police chief	Restaurant owners	Fire chief	Landscapers
Mayor	Tax preparers	Auto mechanics	Limo drivers
Delivery people	Travel agent	Beautician	Manicurist
Masseuse	Printer	Librarian	Painter

You should be starting to get my drift. Many of these people you see regularly (even daily), some irregularly, and some only on special occasions. That's why you should proactively let them know how and what you're doing.

Too many consultants are embarrassed to do this. Why? Either because they think the community around them is irrelevant, or because they believe that it's an imposition on the other party. Yet, insurance agents, Realtors, auto salespeople, and even restaurateurs acquire the preponderance of their clients and customers in this manner.

If it's good enough and effective for them, it's good enough and effective for you. Take the list given here, add to it your personal contacts that might not appear there, and then put a check mark next to each one you've clearly asked for business and referrals over the past six months. I'm betting the number is fewer than five.

That's not a bet in your favor.

CREATING "SOFT" REFERRAL REQUESTS

There are times when you can create referral requests that are somewhat muted, less assertive, and casual. However, one caveat: *I am not suggesting that these are alternatives for those who may be uneasy being more assertive. That is NOT my point. You must be very assertive in pursuing referrals, just as you should be in pursuing business. I'm instead suggesting that there are appropriate times to be a "kinder, gentler" referral pursuer!*

If you're "in the moment," either professionally or personally, when you interact with others, you'll no doubt find opportunities and possibilities where you can suggest a referral. Here are the most common scenarios, but bear in mind that you should adjust my process here to your particular circumstances.

1. The Innocent Mention

Someone mentions to you in the course of other matters that a friend or acquaintance is looking for some kind of help. You have two options here:

- Make a mental note (in a social environment) or a physical note (in a business environment), and return to this when the immediate conversation has ended, but while you're still together (or on the phone). Say, "By the way, if I heard you correctly, Tom needs some assistance getting over his speaking nervousness. I'd be happy to talk to him about it."

- Stop the conversation at the moment the need is mentioned (in a social or business environment); say, "Excuse me, but before I lose that thought . . . "; and then continue with the previous statement.

2. The Mistaken Direction

You find out that someone is actively seeking help. You might hear, "I was talking to Joanne, who's hard to pin down because she's going crazy trying to set up a leadership retreat. . . ."

Then you reply, "You might not realize that I have experience in the area and could probably greatly reduce her time investment and concerns about this. . . ."

3. The Unspoken Need

You're in a meeting, casual or formal, business or social, and there is a recurring issue: a lack of progress, continuing conflict, a lack of planning, or any of a host of other challenges and problems. You suggest the following, "It seems to me we're constantly frustrated by a lack of support from the other group's leader. My specialty is mediation and conflict resolution, and I'd be happy to take this on as a formal project if you think it's at the point where informal approaches aren't going to work. If so, is someone willing to introduce me to Janet, whose budget would be involved in enabling this work?"

4. The Observed Weakness

You find that someone in a key position (e.g., a peer of the buyer, a friend of a friend, or a colleague's colleague) is experiencing an obvious difficulty that is unspoken but can be readily observed. You offer to intervene as someone who is not vested in any particular outcome other than improving that person's condition and performance. You ask, "If you'll simply introduce me and my expertise, I'll be happy to privately pursue whether he will accept help, either overtly or covertly."

5. Between the Lines

You read something in the press, from client sources, or on the Internet that prompts you to believe that a key need is developing. For example, you read that a prominent local firm, because of technology advances, has reorganized and now has 350 excess people. There is great concern about their future.

You know someone who works there, or who once worked there, or who knows someone there, and you ask for an introduction, with the intent of getting yourself in front of a senior executive who would be concerned about the ethical approach and public opinion. You explain to all concerned your skills in assessment, placement, and counseling.

6. The Schmooze

You're sitting in a public area waiting for your car to be serviced (or your hair to be cut or your paperwork to be processed), and you overhear people expressing a need, such as, "The school committee meeting is going to be chaotic again because no one takes charge, the audience simply yells its disapproval, and the acoustics are terrible."

You ask what school meeting they are talking about, who the chairperson is, and whether they personally know that individual, to see if you can at least use their name in making contact, since you are an expert facilitator.

7. The Network

You're at a professional association meeting, and you've learned from past meetings who the real "players" are. You make a point of entering into informal discussions and listening for those situations that they cannot (or choose not to) handle. You request an introduction to the owner of the issue, so that everyone can look good. If you speak to enough of these people at enough meetings, you'll usually find a number of referrals that are inappropriate business for them, but good for you.

8. Reciprocal Obligation

You make a point of learning what others do, assuring yourself of their quality, then referring prospects to them, mentioning your name or through your introduction, which you then follow up on assiduously. If you do this with several people, you will find referrals in reciprocity heading your way. Ensure that your colleagues are successful and experienced so that they *can* reciprocate!

9. The Suggested Improvement

No one is asking for anything, but you see a situation that could be drastically improved through your expertise. You demonstrate to an intermediary (again, in either a business or a social environment) what the dramatic improvement would be. Example: you show someone on the steering committee at your club how to raise funds more effectively and more quickly, and you ask for an introduction to the club president, whom you've never met, on that basis.

10. Serendipity: Do Ask, Do Tell

Examine every relationship for opportunity. (Remember, the mental set is that you have tremendous value that you'd be remiss not to offer.) When we were introduced by a friend to Marshall Goldsmith, the renowned coaching expert, a couple of us asked for some help or favors. He revealed that he had always done the same thing during his career, and he quickly offered his help. (He is a prince of a guy.)

Ask for introductions as a matter of course during your interactions with others as you learn more about them and their contacts. What's the worst that can happen? You certainly can't be any worse off, and you may be a whole lot better off.

Listen Up!

Referral acquisition is a natural fact of business life. Try to build that fact into your everyday activities and relationships, no matter how formal or casual they may be.

Whom can you make a casual inquiry of later today or tomorrow morning who will allow you to experiment and test these approaches? I'll wager that there are a lot more people in that category than you think.

USING SOCIAL AND CIVIC MECHANISMS

Let's focus for a few pages on nonbusiness referrals and "call everyone you know." You're meeting people every day who have the potential to help you, some of whom are obvious and some not.

Civic Positions

I served on our town's planning board for several years, eventually serving as vice chair and then as chair before "retiring." (I could have stayed far longer, but I believe these positions demand regular turnover to create diversity in local government.) We met biweekly, and in the course of my volunteer position, I met

Board members	Attorneys	Engineers
Homeowners	Consultants	Town council members
Police officers	Fire officers	Other board chairs
State representatives	Builders	General contractors
Architects	Landscapers	Designers

You get the idea. This is typical of most of small-town America. In most of these categories, there were the "usual faces" (e.g., this type of law was a specialty, and only a handful of attorneys represented most applicants; the same with engineers).

During the course of a year, I probably met 500 people and became very familiar with 50. They, in turn, learned of my background and my work. (It's a very good idea to Google board members and find out what is likely to influence and persuade their votes.) I didn't need to serve as the chair to gain these contacts and familiarity—there were only eight board members, and the hearings were quite intimate.

This is an excellent vehicle for meeting others, spreading your repute, *and asking for referrals under appropriate conditions.* If you don't think that's possible, just watch the attorneys!

Volunteer Nonprofit Work

I served on the board of a shelter for battered women for a couple of years. As part of my service to the organization, I volunteered my strategy skills so that there wasn't the need to spend money to hire a consultant or seek more funding from external sources.

The strategy retreat, with its preparation and follow-up, wasn't any easier than a for-fee project, but it did showcase my abilities and approaches for the board. I was introduced to the local police chief. He told me that he always had a representative on the board, since a seat was assigned to the police department. He explained that he was seeking relatively rare federal accreditation for his department, and that a strategic plan was a required element.

"Chief," I delicately pointed out, "I'm afraid I can't do any more pro bono work this year."

"Oh, I have a grant that should take care of the fee," he smiled.

I went to work, and that police force is now accredited.

Listen Up!
There are people all around you who can help you. The royal road to that destination is usually to help them, first.

Private Clubs

A great many of us belong to a variety of clubs, some associated with sports (golf or racquetball), good deeds (Lions or Elks), business responsibility (Rotary), education (college), interests (art), dining, and other areas. Most of them are quite easy to join—I'm not talking about 12 references and a souvenir menu from the *Mayflower*. (And I'm always cognizant of Groucho Marx's great observation that he wouldn't want to be a member of any club that agreed to have him as a member!)

Aside from the obvious potential for schmoozing with members and finding people who can help you, there is a much more prominent and less labor-intensive approach in these organizations. It's reminiscent of Mickey Rooney and Judy Garland solving all problems with the admonition, "Let's put on a show!"

My "show" is an enrichment experience. Most of these clubs embrace luncheon speakers (some of them also welcome non-members to speak), members who can host special evenings, and other benefits for the membership. There is often an educational component in the year's planning for these organizations.

Volunteer to provide 90 minutes in a private room on a voluntary basis on your specialty—leadership, communication, investing, safety, whatever. Have the session advertised in the club's newsletter and on its website for at least a month prior to the event.

You may sell someone in the room during your presentation, but more likely you'll create a "buzz" and word of mouth that will reach well beyond your actual attendance. The publicity, the event, and the feedback will create significant referral possibilities.[1]

---

[1] As you've no doubt noticed, many of these referral techniques can also gain you more immediate business, which is why revenue and referrals are equally valuable and intertwined.

CASE STUDY: The Unique Multiplier

We dine out seven nights a week. On a couple of occasions, I'd see a man in the same restaurants whom I didn't know, but whom I recognized. Eventually, he came over to me and said, "Aren't you Alan Weiss? That's your car outside, right?"

We introduced ourselves, and I learned that his name was Joe and that he owned a great deal of local real estate.

We began greeting each other when we met (a couple of times a month), and he introduced us to others in the restaurants, since he seemed to know everyone: the owner of the dealership where we purchased my wife's cars, the owner of the restaurant, city officials, and so forth.

One day, Joe told me that he had gone to my website and was impressed with my credentials, and he asked why I didn't volunteer to lend my expertise to the city. I told him that I had, but I had been turned down repeatedly, told that there were enough "consultants" around, and told that I wasn't even qualified for the sewer commission.

"I'll talk to some people," said Joe.

Two weeks later, I was appointed to the planning board, the benefits of which I've previously explained here!

Joe is a "unique multiplier," someone who isn't himself a buyer, but who can refer people to scores of others, will always get a hearing, and can't be ignored. There are unique multipliers in every community.

Find them!

In these clubs, you have a triple opportunity: serve on a board or committee, network with members, and create an "enrichment" experience. That's a great return on your dues, not even considering the other benefits!

You live in your community every day. There are opportunities all around you. *If* your mental set is that you have tremendous value to provide to people and you must alert them to it, you'll become quite calm and quite adept at using your immediate surroundings as a primary source of referrals.

LANGUAGE TEMPLATE

I've periodically suggested language throughout the book, but I also want to "congregate" it in certain places so that you can ponder it and integrate it into your own style.

Let me repeat: language controls discussion, discussion controls relationships, relationships control business, and the best business consists of both revenue and referrals.

> **Listen Up!**
> *The people who do not obtain referrals are not failing because of lack of opportunity. They are usually failing because of improper language.*

Here are general rules for the best language for referrals, which I'll follow with specific examples:

- Create an expectation early in your discussions; never spring a referral request on a client.
- Accentuate the "three-way win": for the referral source, the referral, and you.
- Focus on value, not increased business.
- Focus on probable reciprocity and appreciation.
- Stress the referrals that your client has received from others as a professional courtesy.
- In nonbusiness settings, focus on the nature of collegiality and mutual assistance.
- Always try to provide options—a "choice of yeses."
- Always try to have a specific date and time for follow-up, if needed.

Here is the language I'd recommend specifically for the philosophy of CEYK in both personal and professional circumstances. Adapt the language as appropriate for the setting, from client to neighbor, from colleague to family member.

Joan, we hadn't spoken in a while before I called you, but I've heard you speak three times now of that executive who is so persuasive one-on-one but who has so much trouble addressing groups. It sounds like it's been going on far too long, and perhaps is impeding his career. Why not introduce me? I think I can probably help him quickly.

Tim, this is Joanne. I read that you had set a record for placements in the month of June. Congratulations! I've tried to send as many people as I can to you. Tell me, which of your clients do you think could best profit from the value I'm providing today, with even more credit accruing to you in the process?

I wanted to make a quick announcement before we break for lunch. I've launched a new service for colleagues and associates of most of you in this room, and I've provided a free sample and demonstration on my website. I'd like you to try it as my advance appreciation of anyone you can recommend who may require these services for his or her own growth.

Tina, I appreciate your willingness to provide referrals, and to make it as simple and painless as possible. Here are the criteria that have worked best for me: a senior vice president or profit center head; someone with stated needs to improve customer service; and someone who is successful and oriented toward stellar growth.

James, I know you don't normally do this, and I greatly appreciate your willingness to consider referrals for me. We can do this in a combination of four approaches, based on your comfort level: a personal introduction; an introduction by phone or mail; permission to use your name; and your permission for selected others to call you. Let's discuss who falls into which category.

Doctor, before I leave, I want to take two minutes to explain the kind of improvement my company is providing for small business owners. I've been very happy to have referred patients to you in the past, and I'd be grateful if you would keep my business in mind for those people who may ask you about issues of growth, valuation, and exit strategies.

Carl, I'm coming in for my tax appointment on the fifth at 10, and I'd like you to set aside an extra 15 minutes at the end so that we can discuss some mutual referral support. I've sent people to you in the past on a random and spontaneous basis, but I'd like to formalize that and perhaps set up the basis for reciprocal referrals.

Wanda, it's amazing to consider that all of the fine work we've done together was made possible by my being referred to you by your cousin, whom I met at our kids' soccer match! But that's happened more frequently in my business than I ever expected. Who do you know among your family, friends, and colleagues whom you'd recommend that I contact, and what role would you be willing to play?

We have more in common in terms of synergy in our businesses than I ever would have suspected. This event tonight isn't the time or the place, but can we select a good time to have lunch or grab coffee to discuss how we might share prospects? I'm around all this week. Do you have your calendar with you?

Jenny, after I speak at your event, what are the chances of your introducing me to your outside board members? I believe there's a reception afterward, and it would be great to have an introduction that provides perspective on the results we've produced during the project.

Peter, the club offers a variety of educational and enrichment events by outsiders. How about one of "our own" doing one? I'd be happy to customize something for the members, since I know them so well. Would you be willing to schedule it and promote it on the club website and in the newsletter that goes out with the monthly billing? I'll provide free books and materials if we can get a minimum of 20 people to attend.

What do you see in this language? You can surmise that these are confident requests, oriented toward benefit, value, and outcomes, not sales or meetings. There is a reliance on a peer-level relationship. There is never embarrassment or obsequiousness.

When you're preparing for a meeting, you can practice the language or even include some of it in your notes and materials for the session. But if you're "in the moment" at a club, event, or chance meeting, you have to be prepared to extemporize. Here are the important elements to always remember:

- *Request.* Make your request apparent and specific.
- *Follow-up.* If it is not possible to pursue this opportunity immediately, establish a specific date and time to follow up. (That means always having your own electronic or physical calendar available. That's easy to do with an iPhone or similar device.)
- *Provide options.* Anticipate that someone may or may not want to be further involved, and minimize any inconvenience or awkwardness through options.
- *Reciprocity.* Where possible, demonstrate what you've already done for this person and/or would be likely to do in the future.
- *Perseverance.* Take the time you need. If necessary, specify in advance that you'll need some extra time.
- *Gratitude.* Send a "thank you" and keep your referral source aware of your progress.

IF AND WHEN TO PAY REFERRAL FEES

In many cases—perhaps in most cases—people make referrals for you without expecting a quid pro quo financial gain. They may certainly expect a "thank you" and the reciprocity that such referrals should entail wherever possible. But your doctor, club buddy, senior management buyer, or similar person usually doesn't expect a lagniappe. (I used to go to a dentist who gave the women a rose when they recommended a new patient. It's the thought that counts.)

Having made this point, there are times—and I've referred to them in Chapter 6—where fees are a consideration. Let's conclude this chapter about contacting everyone you know, professionally and personally, with some guidelines on what can be a sensitive and even infuriating interaction.

First and foremost, the ethics that guide my actions:

1. Never provide any kind of monetary reward (including expensive gifts—that's why the rose is harmless) for organizational employees who are referring you elsewhere, whether within their organization or outside it. Such a gift or payment will often violate organizational policy, but it's not right under any circumstances. You can't pay your client's employees, at any level, for leads or referrals. They should do it at your request or of their own volition based on the quality of your work. The referred party will think that's the reason. This includes providing anything discounted or for free, such as a lower price on a project, a free workshop, complimentary coaching, and so on.

2. Never provide a fee to another consultant (or other professional services provider) who has been asked to find resources and has chosen you (or offers to choose you for a fee). The client believes that the existing consultant's recommendation is based on quality and objectivity, not on financial self-interest. This type of kindness should be repaid with reciprocity where appropriate, but not with cash on the barrelhead. There should be complete transparency in referrals, and that means

embarrassing and inappropriate financial connections would be immediately obvious.

If you agree at all with my ethical stance, then those who remain are people who are not doing business with the referral (although they may know him well). This includes a great many people, most of whom will be excluded from further financial consideration by my first paragraph in this segment.

So how do we deal with those who may both merit and enjoy (or demand) financial consideration, such as

Mutual friends	Professional colleagues
Customers	Analysts
Industry experts	Serendipity

Professionals who no longer conduct business there

My recommendation is that you employ a formula, so that your position is consistent and objective, and is based on the true value provided by the third party only if and when a project is commissioned.

Listen Up!
You won't be paying for most referrals. With those you do pay for, make sure you're saying an appropriate "thank you" and not an inappropriate "here are the keys to my house."

Here are my standards:

- For the name of a buyer with a legitimate need for your value, whom you contact and with whom you create a business relationship: 5 to 10 percent of that project's revenue

- For an introduction in person or by phone or e-mail that hastens your ability to meet a buyer and quickly establish your credibility, and business ensues: 10 to 15 percent of that project's revenue
- For virtually closing the deal and singing your praises, so that you merely need to meet the buyer to consummate the business, 15 to 20 percent of that project's revenue

Note that I recommend a range within which to work; clear criteria for the ranges; payment only on performance; and restricting the payment to that project's initial revenues. This last item is vital, because you should not be paying on repeat business, more referrals, and so on. If the initial business is $100,000

CASE STUDY: The Guaranteed Business in Europe

I received an e-mail from a woman I know who told me to call when I could because she had a great lead for me—the president of Siemens in Europe, the global electronics powerhouse. She said it was "guaranteed." Since she had European roots and connections, I was immediately interested.

When I called her, she told me of needs the president and the company had that required my strategic approaches. Yet she sounded very nebulous, somewhere up around 100,000 feet, and that surprised me, as her con-

versations with him should have been more specific.

"What did he exactly say about expansion?" I asked.

"I don't recall seeing that," she replied.

"Seeing it? What kind of conversation was this?"

"Oh, we didn't talk."

"Then how do you know all of this?"

"I read an article about him in the current issue of *BusinessWeek*."

Lesson: always consider the source.

in category 1, then $5,000 or so is worth paying. But if it's only a speech for $15,000, then $1,000 is more appropriate. Any business you create from that speech is, well, your business.

If you're asked whether you provide referral fees, be somewhat coy. Say that it depends, based upon the quality and the conditions. There are some people who simply throw names out, hoping to get lucky, with you (and others like you) doing all the work. But there will be times—infrequently—when such payments make sense, are appropriate, and may well stimulate more such referrals in the future.

You need to be prepared for all contingencies. Just don't give away the farm to someone who tells you that the sun has risen.

REFERRAL AMMUNITION

ASSEMBLING TESTIMONIALS, ENDORSEMENTS, AND LOVE LETTERS

ASK EARLIER THAN YOU WOULD THINK

Referrals don't exist in isolation; they exist in the dynamic of trusting and mutually beneficial client relationships. Therefore, there is a plethora of synergistic promotional help surrounding them that can be used to stimulate referrals, but that is also valuable in and of itself.

Here is a counterintuitive example: some of the best people to ask for endorsements are *those who did not accept a proposal from you*. Think about this: you've built a trusting relationship; gained conceptual agreement on objectives, metrics, and value; and submitted a proposal with options and a strong ROI. But for some reason, the buyer decided not to go further. (My "hit rate" traditionally has been 80 percent, which means that my proposals are refused 20 percent of the time.)

The buyer may demur because conditions have changed, other priorities have intervened, your proposal is not what he expected, or any other of a host of reasons. The situation can't be salvaged. However, the buyer is apologetic, and honestly regrets that you can't do business together. This is a person with whom you have a trusting relationship.

Ask for referrals!

The buyer will often feel that she "owes" you something at this point, and a referral (or testimonial or serving as a reference) is readily accommodated. (If you're concerned that the buyer can't say you worked together, don't be. You simply need an introduction to other buyers with the endorsement, "Our circumstances don't permit it, but if they did, I would hire him in a second!")

You can't ask much earlier than when a proposal has been rejected!

Listen Up!
You can never be worse off for asking, and you can be a lot worse off for not asking. It's really that simple.

You can be asking for any or all of these promotional aids.

References

Will the buyer serve as a reference to be called by other prospects? Many people prefer not to have something in writing, but to serve in this capacity. Two key rules: you should send only qualified buyers with whom you've developed a relationship to contact your reference, and you should alert the reference first that someone will be calling him. *Never* give references to a nonbuyer, period. Have sufficient references so that you can use each no more than once a quarter. (Trick of the trade: when you're ready, provide a reference sheet of 15 people, three columns of five, filling up one sheet of stationery.

Your prospect will usually opt not to call anyone, whereas if you provide three names, all three will be called. Business psychology 101.)

Testimonials

Many buyers prefer not to be interrupted or to have to respond to phone calls, so a testimonial is easier for them. Keys here: try to get permission to use the testimonial in multiple venues (blog, website, hard copy, and so forth); *always* use the person's full name, title, and company, or the testimonial is worthless— "blind" testimonials (senior manager in a major financial firm) are ludicrous; and always ask for a video as well as a written testimonial. Video testimonials can be done informally with a small camera, need be only 30 to 60 seconds, and can be highly effective (see the discussion of technology in the next segment). Also, make sure you have permission to "update" testimonials should the need arise (newer projects, different title or position, and so on).

CASE STUDY: The Revlon Revelation

Many years ago, I had a wonderful project at Revlon, and the senior vice president who was my buyer—with whom I had a terrific relationship—agreed to give me a testimonial. He was a great guy, but he tended to procrastinate about such things.

After three requests, I stopped by his office one day unexpectedly while I was in New York on other business. I asked his secretary for a copy of his private stationery. She knew me well and provided it.

I wrote a testimonial that would have embarrassed my mother and sent it to him, telling him that if he didn't send a real one, I would forge his name and use the one I had created.

One week later, I had a glowing testimonial.

Endorsements

These are often called "blurbs" and are brief comments for a book jacket, brochure, article, or other promotional material that you are creating. (One trend these days is to have 25 endorsements in the opening pages of a book, which I find tedious and a case of overkill—three great ones on the jacket are far more impressive.) The higher level your buyer's position is and/or the better known she is, the more attractive this option becomes. Name recognition matters most with the general public (as opposed to intimate and personal connections with referrals) for such endorsements.

There is a difference between a business and a character referral (or other promotional aspect), and both are important. The former talks about actual work that you've done together, while the latter addresses your ethics, integrity, longevity, credibility, and so on. Sometimes the former can provide both. But don't overlook the value of the latter. You can derive these from contacts in your social, civic, and professional associations.

All of these support mechanisms from clients and relevant others create a powerful mix, not merely in terms of your own promotion to prospects, but also in terms of generating and perpetuating more of the same support. For example, clients who serve as references may have occasion (you should ensure that they do) to see others' video testimonials on your site and want to be a part of that for their own promotional and ego reasons.

Others may want you to reciprocate, with endorsements of their role in projects, or their firm's role, or their products and services (see coauthoring, discussed later). One of the most overlooked referral techniques—also useful in garnering the other promotional assets discussed here—is *providing referrals, serving as a reference, granting endorsements, and writing testimonials.* The more you give, the more you get. Some people may never say so much as a "thank you" or acknowledge what you've done, but others (most) are quite gracious in reciprocating. Moreover, you will be at the top of the priority list.

You aren't alone in requesting referrals and other promotional support. By providing these "boosts" for others where appropriate, you raise your own stature in terms of their priorities as to whom to help in return.

Thus, as they say about voting in Jersey City, ask early and often! Diversify your requests to include the other aspects of promotion, which will create synergy and allow people additional options when some are inappropriate or prohibited. Accept both business and character referrals. And take the initiative to "give to get."

Now let's examine how to exploit the positive results of this work.

USING TECHNOLOGY TO EXPONENTIALLY IMPROVE IMPACT

Referrals were once made by letter or phone call, or sometimes in person. Testimonials were hard-copy letters that were then copied and sent on to prospects. (I still have my old bound book of testimonial letters that my printer would put together for me.) References were sought by phone or mail.

All of this took a lot of time.

Referrals are turbocharged today because of the Internet and the new informality of business and society. However, bear in mind that personal introductions are *always* superior to all other forms for these reasons:

- E-mail is one-dimensional, without inflection, and with little privacy; it can easily be lost in the overall "noise" of this type of communication.

- Voice mail is two-dimensional and can add emphasis and intonation, but it's also prone to be lost amidst the crowd, and there is no chance to respond or follow up in real time.

- Personal interaction is three-dimensional, and provides for immediate relationship building and follow-up. In my experience, the likelihood of gaining an immediate appointment with a referral done in person, with all three parties present, is over 90 percent. The other two options are 50 percent at best, and that's with a far longer delay.

Having established the primacy of in-person referrals, let's examine how technology can raise the probability of future meetings and business above the norm.

Video Testimonials

We've touched on these throughout the book. You should plan to have two or three on your home page and others spread around your site to touch on relevant topics.

Video Interviews

A third party interviewing your buyer on camera is highly effective (more so than if you do it yourself). These, too, should be brief, but they should allow the buyer not only to sing your praises but to illustrate the results of your work together.

A Podcast or Teleconference Series

You can ask your clients to participate in five-minute mini-interviews or discussions with you that you turn into a "series," running one a month. These can be either passive on your website and blog, or active by your sending them to prospects with your promotional material.

E-mail Signature Files

If you have permission, place a testimonial in your signature file. (Too few consultants use these well in any case—just today I had to ask a woman what her last name is, since it appears nowhere on her e-mail at all!) Place a terrific testimonial line in your signature file, since you're sending out thousands of these potential promotion pieces a month and don't even realize it.

Blogging

In your blogging, include as many war stories and quotes as you can. For example:

> My subject today is distinguishing between teams and committees, which are two different entities requiring two different management approaches. My latest encounter with this need was at Acme, Inc., where senior vice president of operations Herb Chambers noted, "We imagined we had to provide team building until Alan came along in the nick of time and demonstrated that we had no teams to build! He opened our eyes to new management challenges."

This is a key form of reference and testimonial that you can control once you acquire permission to use such quotes. You can see how natural they are in the context of your article. And this is an article that "in the old days" would have had to wait for the mail to circulate it, but that now can be instantly shared on a blog, with commentary from readers and your response to the commentary. You could even include at the conclusion of the article (again, with permission): "If you'd like to contact Herb Chambers and learn more about the identification and need for committees in place of teams, you can use this e-mail address with this article's headline in the subject line."

Listen Up!
You can't include too much information about whom you've worked with and to what ends in electronic vehicles, provided you have permission and you have achieved good ends!

Newsletters

There are a great many electronic newsletters *because with the advent of the Internet, they can be highly targeted and content-rich for a select audience—these people read them.*

You can run a standing column in your newsletter called "war stories" or "success samples" or whatever. These can include names and quotes from clients who would be good sources for others who want to learn more about you. (We'll talk about coauthoring in the pages that follow.)

Don't simply take no for an answer. You're a consultant. Find a way in which your referrals, testimonials, and other endorsements *also* improve your client's condition.

COAUTHORING, COPRODUCING, AND COOPERATING

Some of the most powerful referral ammunition is created when you and your client collaborate. That collaboration can

Digression on Nondisclosure

Many clients will have you sign nondisclosure and confidentiality agreements. Others will severely restrict your ability to use their logos and even their names. In many cases, even senior people are under strict orders to never endorse or provide marketing help for external resources.

There, that's over; it's on the table!

Let me remind you that buyers have egos and companies love publicity. The way to overcome many of these strictures is to paint your client (individual and/or organization) in a dazzling light, within which you are also illuminated. It's worth the wait to get this past legal scrutiny, but that wait can be truncated if a key executive (or several) see a golden opportunity in the publicity.

What kind of publicity would overcome the legal eagles?

- *The publicity may make it easier to attract and retain top talent, cutting recruiting costs.*
- *The firm's community image and reputation could be enhanced, helping with local requests, financial issues, and so forth.*
- *The business would be seen as an industry or professional leader, thereby attracting more investors.*
- *The focus could create a more favorable climate for acquisitions or divestitures.*
- *A previous "black eye" could be pushed into the past with this newer, positive news.*

take the form of a published article, appearances together, joint sponsorships, and so forth.

Clients love good publicity, to such an extent that it can lead them to subordinate rules and policies against endorsing consultants or allowing public use of their names and circumstances. Here are a few examples of how some of my mentor program members have successfully collaborated with clients:

- A jointly written paper on an effective methodology for improving customer response time in peak, seasonal periods. The client did not see a competitive advantage in trying to keep the techniques confidential, since it's hard to keep a secret in the industry. Instead, the client felt it was important to allow its customers to know that it had pioneered the effort. The consultant wrote the article, the client vetted it and obtained legal editing and approval, and, with the weight of the client's name, the piece was published in a major business magazine.

- At an industry conference, the consultant was assured by the organizers that a keynote position would be offered if the consultant's client agreed to also appear. The consultant arranged for a presentation of her own, then a few remarks by the client, then an interview, followed by questions from the audience, all within 60 minutes. They appeared together in the publicity for and from the event, and the session was recorded.

- A consultant asked dozens of clients to appear on his teleconferences as interviewees. Ten agreed, and he proceeded to launch a full year of these offerings, which highlighted his work with these clients, but from the clients' point of view. He opened the sessions to questions at the conclusion. These were full-hour testimonials to the clients' work, which listeners paid to subscribe to, and which were used as both products and marketing pieces.

- Clients were offered a guest column on a consultant's blog, with the offer from the consultant of editing and polishing, as needed. They were given templates to use if they needed help. The consultant found that many clients saw such vehicles as aids in their own careers, in certain academic pursuits, and in simply catering to ego.

Listen Up!

Clients often don't want you to use their name or situations, but they are usually very interested in inexpensive publicity that places them in advantageous competitive positions. It's not what's in it for you, it's what's in it for them!

- When she found that her client was heavily engaged in a national effort to raise funds for research to combat a disease, the consultant offered to be the "point person" in her own hometown, and served on the client's steering committee to set strategy for the efforts. Her photo and information appeared in the literature that was sent out, and she attended the fund-raising and volunteer sessions.

- During the client's meeting with customers, which lasted for two days in a convention atmosphere, the consultant readily accepted an invitation to explain why his client was so innovative and what that had meant for improved service to the client's customers. The consultant readily did this for free, and was mobbed by attendees after the session.

CASE STUDY: Atlantic Electric

At one point, this major utility—whose customers include the hotels and casinos in Atlantic City—asked me to help it with downsizing. Normally, I don't do that type of work,[1] but this was necessitated by technology advances that were making too many "old-line" jobs redundant.

What we agreed to do was to place every single person affected. We went to every division of the company to try to fill vacancies with the existing workforce. Then we created a booklet of résumés and supporting information and had the utility executives send it to their counterparts in every organi-zation in the area. Finally, we created a generous early retirement package.

As a result, every single person was either placed or retired. There was virtually zero ill will, which was especially important to the people who remained and from whom high morale and high performance were needed.

My point is that even in the course of a project, you can collaborate and coproduce with clients in dramatic ways, exposing your talent and reputation to countless others with your current client's explicit or tacit endorsement.

[1] Because it's too often a cost-cutting measure that hurts the innocent victims of corporate errors and folly.

You might think that many of these techniques would be more properly seen as marketing tactics. You'd be correct in your identification of them, but I have a specific reason for raising them here, and in this book.

I've continually established that referrals (and related testimonials, references, endorsements, and so on) are as *important* as revenue at the moment. You can look at fees as current revenue and referrals as future revenue. If you can obtain them concurrently, you're maximizing your ROI from any one client.

Consequently, your ability to engage in what may logically seem like marketing activities is actually a simultaneous attempt to build your referral base while delivering value during the course of a consulting project (or any professional services relationship). What you must bear in mind is that a client isn't merely a person or organization for whom you are providing certain "deliverables." A client constitutes a relationship that should be "mined" (I love the word *exploited*, but you may not) for as much present and future income as possible.

That's why you must interact only with true buyers, for example. Lower-level people are interested only in the deliverables and can't provide the referrals and relationships you need in any case. That's why you need to begin "seeding" these ideas from the beginnings of your work with your clients. Not only do you want them prepared, but you never know when the opportunities for cosponsorship, coauthoring, and so on may present themselves.

Think of yourself as constantly collaborating with your clients, especially your key buyers, so that they become inured to your suggesting certain joint efforts. That's impossible if you don't see yourself as a peer of the buyer, and if you don't conduct yourself as an equal of the buyer.

LANGUAGE TEMPLATE

Here is some more suggested language, this time using this chapter's contents and methodology. Language is everything in referral "ammunition," assuming that you've done a great job and your buyer and key client reference points are delighted. Ammunition is wasted if you don't have the opportunity for publicity and/or if you're too timid to use it.

In that omnipresent spirit of having great value and the obligation to share the results of that value with others, consider these gambits:

I'd like to ask you for an early favor that will surface later. Would you consider—when we both believe it to be appropriate—a video testimonial for my website and my blog? I ask now because I realize that there may be legal permissions required, and I wanted to set the stage for what so many of my best clients have done.

Notes: "Painting people into the picture" is very powerful, so the more buyers who have agreed to do this for you, the more you'll be able to get in the future. The first ones are always the toughest and most important. Also, you want to know early if there will be a legal issue so that you can prepare for other alternatives that will be more acceptable to the client. I'm reminded of the famous call home by a daughter in her freshman year at college to her stunned parents. "I'm experimenting with cocaine, have been arrested for drunk driving, lost the gold pendant you gave me, and the guy I was seeing was sent back to prison, but not before he got me pregnant. Just kidding! But I did flunk chemistry . . ." (So if the video is turned down, perhaps coauthoring a paper will be a walk in the park!)

There is a major industry conference scheduled for 16 months from now. I had intended to approach the association's executive director to speak on the very interventions and results we're going to be engaged in here. Is this something that might appeal to you? I can mention your possible involvement, but not guarantee it. This could range from not mentioning the company at all to your copresenting with me. If the latter is of any interest, why don't I run a proposal by you first, and you can put the time aside on your calendar.

Note: When I first started speaking professionally, major conferences were sometimes scheduled two years in advance in terms of content, presenters, and themes. Today, it's often less than a year (although the dates are set far in advance). You want to pique your buyer's interest, introduce the idea, and demonstrate that you'd do the legwork, but also clear the date. In these cases, ego and public acknowledgment may be important factors for both the client organization and the buyer, especially if media will be covering the event.

The *Harvard Business Review* has consistently published the results of organization change efforts when the organization and the consultant have collaborated on the piece. The same is true of the *Sloan Management Review*. The *Wall Street Journal* doesn't accept such articles, but it will assign a reporter to create a piece on a dramatic corporate change or turnaround. I have some samples here. I'm thinking that this might be great publicity for you and the company, and I'd be willing to try to put it in motion and put things together. Should I pursue this?

Note: These high-profile names will generally get a company's attention. Someone in the media told me once that when an investigative show such as *60 Minutes* does an *unfavorable* piece on a firm, its stock price goes *up* the next day in most cases! The focus and attention are highly valuable, especially in the context of an intelligent, proactive improvement. You can't buy this kind of publicity. But put it in motion with the client's permission early, because you want to strike while the project is current and the results are contemporary. Make that case to your buyer, as well.

Why don't we present the progress and the results of the project together during the quarterly divisional meeting? Everyone will be present, we can give a uniform message, and we can answer questions in real time. I think it will place the results in a proper priority, and we can publicly recognize those who were instrumental in our progress and also force the reluctant ones to get on board the ship.

Note: I appeared on stage at Avon with a divisional vice president in front of her 400 people. It was extremely successful, and I was fortunate in that she was a natural presenter and our styles meshed. You may have to make allowances for buyers who aren't great speakers or who tend to see such meetings in narrow terms. But the absolute key for you is that these meetings almost always have outsiders who are potential referrals for you, and they can see you and your buyer both waxing eloquent about a project that has such public notice. I've never walked off a stage like this without people asking me to stop by to see them, or asking the buyer to introduce me.

What would you think about an ongoing interview with me that I'd put in a podcast as the project progressed? We could keep a "real-time" record of our work, and I'd be happy if you used this internally to apprise people of our progress and needs. I'd use it on my blog to inform my community about how a project such as this one unfolds. Naturally, we'd hide any confidential details, and you'd have the final editing option.

Note: If you don't ask, you don't get. Why not create something that both you and the buyer can use in slightly different ways? The buyer can create internal publicity and an automated device to keep people informed of what to expect and how best to participate. You can obtain a narrative of how your methodology unfolds to create dramatic results working as a partner of the buyer. Ten minutes once a week would be a fine start.

Through these language templates, I've tried to provide you with sample language to apply to create referrals, various types of endorsements, and all kinds of support. The language is similar to what you might use in other marketing situations, but here it is specifically directed toward referral business. Remember our fundamental sequence: *language controls discussion, discussion controls relationships, relationships control business.*

You can see that referrals are often directional, with you asking for them and the buyer providing them. But they are also often indirect, with your appearance with the buyer, collaboration, coauthorship, cosponsorship, and other aspects of an excellent relationship demonstrating to others how good you are.

Referrals, and the associated promotional potential that surrounds them, are therefore far more than simply, "Can you give me three names?" The technique that Hal Mapes used (which I described in the first chapter of this book) works on a very basic level, almost in a commodity transaction. ("Can I have three?" "I can give you two." "Can I have them today?" "Check with me next week.")

What we've built so far, three-quarters of the way through the book, is a far more sophisticated, integrated, and continual referral flow. You are laying the groundwork, looking for opportunities, suggesting many alternatives, and even setting up "referral by association"!

Adjust the language I've suggested to suit your own style, clients, and business. But start talking. Make these approaches a habit with every client. You can always stop if you think the results or the circumstances become inappropriate. But if that's the case on many of your engagements, then you have an entirely different problem, don't you?

KEEPING CURRENT WHILE SHOWING CONSISTENCY

If you are diligent and consistent, some of the promotional material you gather from happy clients will grow old. So long as you continue amassing these nuggets, that's not a problem.

But what should you do with the older material? Do you want endorsements and testimonials that are clearly several years old? What about references where the individual's contact information is different? (One consultant I know was embarrassed when a prospect informed him that a reference he called had retired five years previously.)

Here are some guidelines to consider as your "vault" of these assets gets filled:

- For references, check at least annually to ensure that they are current. That includes title, phone, e-mail, and, of course, company affiliation.

- For testimonials in hard copy, I suggest you establish a booklet, which your local printer can assemble. Place the testimonials in chronological order (copies are fine, but on letterhead) to demonstrate consistent quality and high marks from clients over a long period of time. Keep very current testimonials (those from the past year) separate in your press kit, but provide the booklet for added continuity and evidence of continual excellence. Eventually, place the past year's testimonials in the booklet. You don't want the entries to suddenly end five years ago!

- For electronic testimonials, use current ones throughout your website as appropriate, but also create an archive where older ones are stored and prospects can access them. It's a good idea to have excerpts from *all* your testimonials rotate on your home page so that they don't take up too much space, but there is constant evidence of customers' delight.

- For video testimonials, try to avoid references to calendar time when they are recorded. If you can do this, they have tremendous staying power (assuming that no one is wearing bell bottoms or Nehru jackets). But you will have to change them if the subjects change companies or retire. You can establish a video archive, as well.

In general, the higher the level of the source and the better known the company, the more you can perpetuate these testimonials even if someone retires or changes jobs. A CEO of a Fortune 500 company is going to have high impact no matter what's changed (unless she's been arrested!), since at the time she worked with you, she was moved to endorse your work.

So there is a nice blend of staying current but also demonstrating consistency in the quality of your work over time. The only problems you may encounter are when there are inexplicable, long gaps or a sudden end to your testimonials. That's why you should assiduously pursue these testimonials throughout the tenure of your client engagements.

As you acquire more and better clients, don't feel that you can let up on the acquisition of referrals, references, and endorsements. It's easier than ever to obtain them in those cir-

> **Listen Up!**
> *A prospect will be happy that current clients are happy with you, but he will be delighted that you can demonstrate that happiness over many years.*

cumstances, and you should no more refuse to seek them than you would refuse to accept the fees from current clients. Fees and referrals are equally important in your work: one is present tense, the other future tense.

If and when your key contacts change positions, you can request permission to update their information. For example, a change of title and/or location would be simple. However, contacts who change companies create challenges. After all, the testimonial was for your work at the former firm. So, barring the fact that you might work for the new firm, you'll want to be able to say "former chief operating officer" or "former director of national sales."

CASE STUDY: Shameless Promotion

When I gathered about 50 testimonial letters to place in a booklet, I realized that there was so much power in them that a simple compilation would not have all the leverage I sought.

Thus, I created a four-color cover, with copies of my book jackets around the perimeter of the cover, and my photo in the center. And the cover read, "Shouldn't you listen to the man whose advice is valued and heeded by clients in over 50 countries?" I found that prospects would give this a cursory look, raise their eyebrows, and continue with the conversation. They seldom read even a page or asked for a single reference. And they were all happy to be in the book themselves, alongside peers they respected.

That's some of the potential you have with a booklet like that, or with your videos, or any other device where you have a volume of support.

If someone has retired, you can say, "John Jones, Vice President of R&D, now retired," or "former Vice President of R&D John Jones." You can also say, with permission, "Jane Sanders, former Vice President of Acme, now CEO of Global."

Beware of the following:

- *Poor publicity.* That applies not just to your endorser, but to the firm. After the breakup of Andersen, I stopped using its endorsements. I wasn't comfortable with the public perception of the firm and its connection to Enron, even though the work I had done for it was in an entirely different area.

- *Changing times.* I don't think it would be hugely helpful to have three dozen vacuum-tube manufacturers attest to your prowess, unless you have transistor people in there as well! Working for the vinyl record people is not necessarily a plus, despite your outstanding work.

- *Firms that were great when you were there, but aren't so great any more.* If you read the iconic *In Search of Excellence*, you'll find that many of those stellar examples at the time have since fallen on quite hard times. The nature of their mediocre performance today can easily overwhelm the brilliance of your efforts when they were stars years ago.

Keep your supporting accolades current while also creating a rich history. You can't go wrong with evidence of long-term success.

YOU CAN GO HOME AGAIN—REVISITING PAST CLIENTS

HEY, AREN'T YOU . . . ?

MAINTAINING CONTACTS

By this time, you must be thinking, "How do I make sure that all these valuable contacts remain valuable contacts?" Well, no worries; you'll do better than I did, at least when I was starting out!

Computers were a minor issue even in the mid-1980s, and a PDA or cell phone was as unrealistic as Dick Tracy's wrist radio in the comics. (Today, of course, my iPhone is better than his wrist radio.) Consequently, information was captured the old-fashioned way—by writing it down.

I found it so laborious to keep details in my notebook about whom I met that I stopped doing it, on the assumption that I'd be in constant contact with clients in any case, and the rest didn't matter. Bad assumption. A lot of you are making this same assumption even though you have the electronic means in your briefcase to access more information in a minute than I could in a week in 1985, when I began my practice.

This is a bad assumption; you have to capture the name and contact information of everyone *who is of potential consequence* because

- You will forget them.
- They don't always become clients, and you won't see them as continually as you thought you would.
- Client engagements eventually end.
- Someone who is not of immediate interest can become of immense interest later on.
- You may have nothing to suggest at the time, but as you evolve, you may be able to suggest something later.[1]
- You will forget them.

Listen Up!
Sometimes you know immediately who can help you and how. Sometimes you do not. And sometimes the conditions change, so that someone who was once of little relevance is now of great relevance.

Once again, you'll find that many of these dynamics apply to potential clients as well as to referrals and promotion, and that's because *every* prospect has the dual and concurrent potential to be both a client and a referral source.

When I speak of *potential consequence*, I mean DO capture the following people's information:

---

[1] For example, a year later you may have had a book proposal accepted by a publisher and need endorsements, for which someone you met would be a perfect candidate.

- Buyers, whether or not they've actually become clients
- Key recommenders
- Media sources, such as editors, reporters, and talk show producers
- Key buyer subordinates
- Key implementers for the projects
- Executives you meet in the course of your work with a client, even though they are unrelated to the client
- Professional and trade association officers
- Community leaders
- Social contacts in key positions

Note that the list deliberately includes not only those who can purchase or refer you at the time, but also those who will be able to purchase or refer you *in the future*. The buyer's top subordinate will probably become a buyer at some point; the city council member might be elected to the state senate (as I write this, a local mayor was elected to the U.S. Congress).

Some contacts will disappear because they retire, pass away, move to nonrelevant positions, are fired, or simply drop out of sight. If you start with a static list of only those who are currently helping you, then you're limited to replacing the attrition with new and future contacts. But if you carefully identify and record all those in potential categories, you'll also be able to replace attrition with previous contacts who have "grown into" positions where they are high-potential supporters.

(I'm not trying to be mercenary, but countries have to have a birth rate that replaces their death rate, or they must import labor. Otherwise, they'll suffer declining productivity through unfilled jobs and lack of expansion. You're the head of your own country, and we're talking about your referral population!)

To keep this manageable, those with potential consequence would not, for example, include

- Gatekeepers.
- Human resources, training, and learning and
  development personnel.
- Subordinates and implementers who are not destined
  for greater things.
- Social contacts who do not hold relevant positions.
- People who have reacted badly to you or whom you
  do not like. (Life is too short to deliberately deal with
  unpleasant people when you don't have to.)
- People you happen to meet, no matter how nice, who
  simply are not in relevant positions.

You're probably asking now, "How do I know whether
someone might or might not accede to a 'relevant position'?
Can't a human resources person transfer out and become
senior vice president of strategy?"

Yes, but.

You have to draw the line somewhere, and you'll dilute
your lists and contacts *and your communications options* (we'll talk
about them later) if you are indiscriminate in the lists you maintain. You can always create a triage of high potential, moderate
potential, and questionable potential if you don't trust me on
this. But if you're disciplined in capturing the names of highly
relevant people, you'll have plenty to work with.

This was the biggest mistake I made in my consulting
career, and the lack of technology was no excuse. I simply paid
correct and close attention to closing business immediately, but
not enough attention to creating future business. While I was
fortunate to attract referrals through my blue-chip clients, writing, and speaking, I want to emphasize the word *fortunate*.

Why leave your fate to fortune? You can accelerate your progress by gathering as much contact information as possible and using it now and in the future. You may or may not have the writing and speaking opportunities I've had, but you definitely can have the referral reality if you address this as a fundamental part of your business.

So, whether by PDA, iPad, Filofax, business card, laptop, marginal note, corporate brochure, or tattoo, make sure you accurately capture the name, rank, serial number, and complete contact information of all relevant people. Then deposit it in the (data) bank that contains your highest-level return on investment.

TRACKING KEY PEOPLE

There is so much talk about databases today that I've found people who never actually contact anyone; they have no time, since they're constantly tending to the care and feeding of their databases. Silver Mine, Consistent Communication, Email Ecstasy—you name it.

So what's the best way to "track" people? How do you know where they go? Unlike the case of a big game hunter, looking for spoor probably isn't the answer here.

The best way is to do this on an ongoing basis automatically. What would automatically tell you that someone has moved or changed contact information? In this transitory business environment, that's more common than ever. When I was young, for most people it was one job until retirement. They had one phone number and one physical address. Today, the likelihood is four or more jobs post-college, and a multitude of numbers for phones, addresses for e-mail, and assorted texts, social media platforms, and other "hangouts."

So, in no particular order, here are some methods.

Talk to Them Often

If you have a list on which you've performed some triage as suggested previously, try to talk at least to your very top third on a regular basis. Provide them with value, share insights, ask for advice—it doesn't matter. This kind of constant contact will probably result in their telling you ahead of time when they are moving or changing their information in any way. (Every decent call center asks every person ordering to reconfirm his contact information, even if he's called the day before and has a long-standing account. This is just good business in terms of the value of customer contact.)

Create Automated Lists

This is as simple as making sure all of your contacts (at any of the triage levels) receive frequent mailings. Those might include a newsletter, a promotional mailing, a brief weekly note, and so forth. Your list service or your own software will alert you to bounced e-mails. This is your prompt to follow up and find out what happened. (Sometimes the software will actually give you the new address.) It's sometimes after the horse has scooted from the barn, but the more frequent these mailings are, the quicker you'll know of movement. As of this writing, I provide the following to my entire contact list in one form or another:

- Balancing Act® newsletter (free, monthly)
- Alan's Monday Morning Memo® (free, weekly)
- Million Dollar Consulting™ Mindset newsletter (free, monthly)
- Alan's Friday Wrap™ (for a fee, weekly)
- Workshop promotion notices (free, monthly)

- Mentor newsletter (free, monthly)
- Weiss Advice (for a fee, monthly)
- Teleconference series (for a fee, monthly)

As you can see, as a solo practitioner, I have all my contacts covered, often in many concurrent vehicles. And when they move, I know it very quickly. In addition, all of these devices have automated address change features (and they accompany an automated "unsubscribe," which is required by antispam laws), so that people are often updating their whereabouts without my even being aware of it. This means that if your contact in your convention e-mail database or iPhone list fails, you can simply search for the name in the appropriate vehicle and see if anything has changed. While you're providing value to people, they're keeping you abreast of where to find them!

The best way to "cleanse" a list is to keep mailing to it. You will routinely receive information about connections who "unsubscribed," were "removed after three bounces," and so on.

Listen Up!
The best way to track your contacts is to have them track you!

Create Gravity, and Then Provide Update Ease

Create value that people visit (as opposed to something that you send them). The most typical example is a blog that has frequent new postings of high import that others quote. Keep an "update my address" option very visible. You may include "for our special offers" or some other inducement. This can also be done on your website.

Use the Social Media Platforms

One of the few marketing advantages of the social medial platforms is that they can provide information on where people are.
Most of your own database options will offer the opportunity
to include LinkedIn or Facebook or whatever. Few people are
involved in changes that alter their online presence and contacts as well as their physical contact information, so this can
be an effective backup. I'd advise this for the upper third or, at
most, two-thirds of your triage list.

Request That People Place You on a
Favored List to Avoid Filters

When I mail out, for example, a 10,000-subscription newsletter, I will get back a half-dozen or so spam filter demands that
I jump through hoops to prove I'm who I claim to be. I always
ignore these at the risk of losing subscribers because they are
too labor-intensive and sometimes result in my receiving solic-
itations from the spam filter companies. (These are generally
new subscribers who haven't bothered to approve my mailings.)
Simply ask that you be placed on a "white list" or approved list
so that spam filters don't kick in.

Always Try to Obtain Personal Information

For the upper reaches of your lists, try to secure personal e-mail
addresses, cell phone numbers, and even home numbers. This
is very possible if you're providing the same information to key
clients and executives. I simply say, "There will be times when
it's urgent that we can reach each other without intermediaries,
so here are my cell phone and home numbers." All of this
depends on your having achieved a trusting relationship with

your buyer. But it's also the platinum insurance that you can always track that person.

I tend to use listservs, which are automated and inexpensive, and which operate 24/7. I can enter information manually, they accept information automatically, I can make list backups, and so forth. For a mailing of 15,000 names, they seldom cost more than $45 per usage, and I tend to send at an early morning hour when Internet traffic is low. (One woman actually asked me how I could send out Balancing Act at 2 in the morning, since that didn't sound "balanced" to her!)

Whatever you do, take pains to monitor and update information about the people on your lists, no less than you track incoming checks and make sure they are deposited in the correct bank account.

Building Databases

The last thing in the world I want to do here is to give technical advice, since that's been one of two areas I've steered well clear of in my consulting endeavors.[2] So accept the following in the spirit in which it's given: you deserve some direction in terms of what I've found successful for me and those I coach, and you're free to disagree and build still better solutions.

But bear in mind Occam's razor: the easiest path is usually the best. You can spend all your time building databases of sterling quality and bulletproof backup while never, along the way, actually attempting to contact anyone on them!

What's the point (the objective) of a database to begin with?

---

[2] The other being finance, since both subjects bore me to tears, no doubt a character flaw on my part.

- To create a repository of information of referral and endorsement clients and prospects that can be amended at any time
- To establish priorities (the triage, as I've termed it) in terms of both quality and nature of the potential
- To enable easy access to and use of the information
- To permit multiple uses, such as for individual contact situationally, for mass distribution of newsletters, for targeted contact for geographic events, and so on
- To safeguard valuable assets, including backup

How often would you access a database?

- Daily, 24 hours a day, people can be automatically subscribing, unsubscribing, or making changes to those aspects that control the material that they receive.
- Weekly, you would be manually entering or deleting contacts as appropriate in the normal course of your own communications and activities.
- Situationally, you would be making changes for special promotions and advisories, such as new programs, accolades, visits to certain locales, and so forth.

Thus, databases can be built automatically through subscription and others' voluntary participation (usually by submitting at least their name and e-mail address) because of an offer you provide. Some consultants' websites provide free downloads and other value if the visitor "registers" with her e-mail address and her name. (I don't like this particular practice, since it clearly implies that the information will be used and discourages some people from signing up. Yet this is the upper left of the Accelerant Curve I described earlier in the book. It's best to provide free stuff without obligation, and request contact information as the individual is attracted to more and more sophisticated offerings.)

> ### Listen Up!
> *If you add 10 names to your database, voluntarily or automatically, every business day, you will have added about 2,500 names in a year. In a couple of years, assuming you raised the daily number through valued offerings, you'll have a five-figure database, at least.*

It is relatively simple, in the course of just a few years, to build a *high-quality* five-figure database. I'm emphasizing *high quality* for the following reason. Think of the market value bell curve from Chapter 2, which I've reprinted in Figure 8.1.

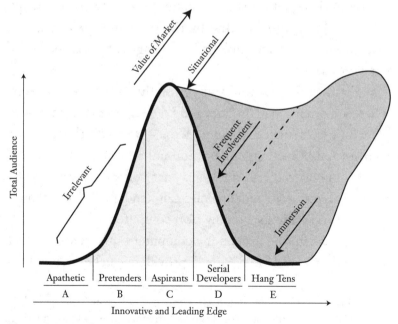

Figure 8.1 Market Value Bell Curve Revisited

You'll recall that the serial developers and "hang tens" are the critical groups. It's best to reach a higher percentage of these smaller but more important markets than a larger percentage of the markets to the left.

Hence, one of my smaller databases has only about 4,000 names. *But every person on it has purchased a product, attended a workshop, or engaged in some other experience with me, and has invested the money to do so.* How powerful is a list like this? Well, the experts usually consider a "good" return (purchases) from an average list to be about 1 to 1.5 percent. But my lists produce results *exceeding 10 percent!*

That means a great deal when you're asking for referrals, endorsements, references, new business, or anything else. (Remember, revenue and referrals are equally important.) So the better your list (and your triage), the less expense, better results, and faster positive action you're going to achieve.

Once you have your own criteria for what you want to keep and where, let me suggest some specific mechanics, while acknowledging the fact that by the time you read this, you may be able to produce holographic images of your lists inside your retina.

First, find a reliable source for the automated aspects. These are often called *listservs*, and I'd get references from people who use them successfully.[3] Do *not* try to do this on your own software or e-mail application unless you are a technical expert, and even then I'd suggest that you stop wasting your time on things that someone else can handle for you. I would then back up these lists on my own computer.

I'd back up the lists on my computer both on an external drive and on one of the "cloud" providers (such as Mozy), so

---

[3] For example, I use databack.com, run by Byron Lunz, which is highly reliable and inexpensive. I have no financial interest in this firm whatsoever; that's just a suggestion from me to you.

that your lists are not dependent on any one location, and so that they are preserved in case your listserv fails, or your computer fails, or the cloud somehow fails.

Then I'd install an instant sync service. My favorite as of this writing is Dropbox, which instantly takes the words I'm now writing on this page and syncs them with my laptop, iPad, and iPhone (and vice versa for all those platforms). This means that if I'm traveling (or even just sitting in another room away from the main computer), I can access a totally up-to-date database.

Finally, having accomplished all this, whether by listening to me or to someone who's technically more proficient, you're ready to form one of the most powerful referral networks of all, one that is not possible until you have these databases built and functioning: the virtual community.

CREATING COMMUNITIES

There is no doubt in my mind that traditional trade associations are going to either metamorphose or die. The ancient ritual of a monthly magazine, a noninteractive website, and an annual conference will become as obsolete as the Mayan calendar. Not even the Mayans are using it any more.

What is currently taking the place of trade and professional associations is communities, comprising those with vested interests in the subject matter and/or the direction of the profession or business.

These communities began when some disgruntled customers took advantage of the Internet and began Web sites called something like AcmeCompanySucks.com (presumably a charter member was Wile E. Coyote[4]). Customers would com-

---

[4] If you've never seen a Road Runner cartoon, you've missed a seminal phenomenon in American humor.

plain, compare notes on their mistreatment at the hands of the corporate monolith, and recommend the best actions to take to overcome corporate sloth, organize boycotts, and deprive the transgressor of business. These were passionate, rabid sites. (Some years ago, I posted a blog article about the shipper UPS and its unfair demand for $100 deposits in return for monthly billing, which were never returned. I received hundreds of responses from . . . disgruntled UPS franchise buyers who took every opportunity to knock the company's treatment of them.)

The smart executives formed their own websites for their organizations and invited customers and clients to comment there, no matter how negative the post. That enabled the organizations to

- Demonstrate a willingness to listen.
- Understand the flaws in their own services and repute.
- Correct legitimate errors on their part.
- Squelch rumors that were untrue.
- Indicate where customers could improve their own experiences.
- Create far better customer relations.
- Provide for positive customer comments and endorsements, which are ongoing, tacit referrals and references.
- Indicate where current strengths can be further exploited.
- *Improve sales in the process of running the community.*

The bromide is that it's always better to know who and where your "enemies" are. These kinds of communities actually embrace them and create positive experiences.

When a repairperson comes to my office to fix my computer, the first action he takes is often to Google the problem, tap into the proper Internet community, and find out what's been reported and already done, so as not to reinvent the wheel. You and I can go there ourselves and find reviews of hardware and software, or of phones, or briefcases, or hotels. There's an Apple-oriented site I visit that informs readers of when the company is likely to introduce upgrades and new products, so that you can plan your buying around them and not purchase the end of the old line.[5]

Thus, these communities offer tremendous value and pragmatic help, under the auspices of the organizations, *but in the delivery of customer-to-customer communication and advice as well.* The value derived accrues to the organizer, though the organizer may or may not intervene frequently. I think you can begin to see how traditional associations (American Institute of Architects, American Bankers Association, Institute of Management Consultants, American Bar Association, and so on) will have to migrate to that kind of customer/client interactivity to stay relevant.

Why should I be content with monthly or annual interaction when I can have it at my fingertips daily?

I've made a point of establishing my own communities, particularly on the right side of Figure 8.1. My goal is to have people talking 24 hours a day at some point somewhere on the globe. These communities effectively "time-shift" comments and responses, so that within a day, one can receive or give advice regardless of one's hemisphere and time zone. The degree to which I interact is my decision, but the value of the experience is always allotted to belonging to the communities I've formed.

[5] As of this writing, it's located here: http://guides.macrumors .com/Buyer%27s_Guide_%28time-ordered%29.

These communities create *huge* referral potential, because people who have experienced your value in a variety of ways suggest to others that they "must" also partake of certain opportunities. The more that happens, the more I create subcommunities.

For example, Alan's Forums (http://www.alansforums .com) contains "right-side" members. (They are there for free if they have joined many of my programs, but others pay $495 for lifetime membership. You can visit and read many posts to test the site at the URL given here.) The discussion boards on the site are variously

- Open to everyone
- Restricted to those with certain past experiences
- Restricted to those with certain types of membership

If someone has access to all the boards, that would mean that she is in "total immersion" in my communities in the chart, which is the natural progression. Every day, people on that forum are "selling" my services to one another by comparing notes on what they've been through, how to use the tools, how they've been successful (communities are great for getting strokes), and so forth. These virtual communities become real communities when people decide to get together in person (I have dozens of these occurring with no participation from me at the time), or when they suggest an experience that I create.

Listen Up!
There is no limit to the number of communities you can set up, and the more they overlap, the more self-reinforcing and growth-oriented they will be.

The reason that I can create "guaranteed" workshops is that the critical mass for success has already formed in one of my communities, in terms of both relevant topics and the number of people required to launch the workshop successfully and begin marketing it to noncommunity members!

My suggestions for forming virtual and real communities are

- Find and retain technological expertise. Don't attempt to do the technical stuff yourself. You want sophistication (search engines, automatic subscription) and a high-quality image.

- Go there often. Let people know you're present. Contribute when you have something important to say or when you need to correct someone else. I visit my main communities about five times a day, and the cumulative time is less than 45 minutes.

- Use the "app" approach. The more valuable people you attract, the more they will attract other people (like the iPhone and apps and app writers). Never worry about giving things away for "free" in terms of your intellectual property. Attract people, and they will come—with others.

- Create a diversity of topics and alternatives for participation so that there is something for everyone (we have boards that include "sex, religion, and politics" for example).

- Encourage subcommunities that can "talk up" experiences and options for others to avail themselves of.

- Run your ideas past the community and encourage its members to create solid, highly supported options for your future offerings. Give community members discounts. (I always give full "scholarships" to those who suggest a new offering that is successfully launched.)

- Publicize the communities and include them for free in high-priced products or services you provide.

Creating multiple communities around the right side of your bell curve, no matter who is in that audience for you (bankers, Realtors, middle managers, professors, insurance brokers, reporters, and so on) will create ongoing referrals while you sleep. There is no better rest than that.

UTILIZING PAST CLIENTS IN CURRENT PROMOTIONS

As you become more and more successful, you'll create a wake of happy clients behind you. However, if you're not careful (or if you don't appreciate their value, as I didn't at first), you'll allow the wake to dissipate and disappear.

Bill Parcells, the football coach and executive, said, "Once you win a Super Bowl, it's yours forever. They can never take that away from you." Once you have a client, that client is in your experience forever. As I tell people in my Mentor Program, "You're always in the Mentor Program. Whether you're active or not is another matter entirely."

Thus, I wouldn't talk so much about "past clients" and "present clients." I'd just talk about "clients." When you create a client list, I wouldn't put an asterisk next to those who are no longer active, remove past clients from the list, or make separate lists of "active" and "inactive" clients!

A client is a client, now and forever. The money in the bank is always good; it doesn't become obsolete, both because money is eternal and because it's not physical, it's a representation made good by your bank. There is no money in the vault marked "Jane's $100,000." If you need the money, the bank will give it to you out of what's on hand.

The same is true of clients. They are always "good"; they don't become obsolete *if you have the right attitude about them and their value.*

Listen Up!
Current clients are money to be invested; past clients are money that is already in the bank. They are worth the same.

Here's how to use that "money in the bank" in terms of current promotion and referral sourcing:

- Keep in touch with them in two ways:
  - *Aggressively.* Contact high-potential past clients with new offers, new value, and new ideas. Find reasons to give them a call.[6]
  - *Passively.* Make sure these buyers and other key people are on your newsletter, podcast, and other lists. Offer them free subscriptions in those instances where you're charging others.
- Keep their written testimonials in place so long as they are in context (for example, if they are from years ago, they should be part of a continuing sequence of accolades, as discussed earlier) and the identification is still accurate. Otherwise, update the contact information ("former CFO of . . .").

[6] Calls are always better than e-mail, as discussed throughout the book. Also, these tactics are effective for repeat business as well as referral business.

- Keep their video testimonials in place. If you must, change the voice-over introduction ("former CFO of . . .").
- Keep the client organization on your client list.
- Keep using them as references for as long as they are willing to serve in that capacity.
- Use the triage technique on them, as well, and ask the top tier for referrals at least twice a year, just as if they were current clients and current buyers.

Now, here are some outré ideas that you may not have thought practical, but that I can assure you will pay referral dividends:

- Invite past buyers to your current marketing events and "seed" the audience with these previously delighted clients. Let them "soft sell" for you by endorsing what you did for them and demonstrating how that would work for others. These may be formal presentations or informal discussions during breaks and social activities. (Interesting question: if you had two critical prospects playing golf, and you couldn't be there, which two people would you most like to pair up to make that foursome?!)
- Consider holding events *solely* for your past clients, as a continuing sign of your appreciation of your work together. These can't be bribes (unless the clients are retired!), so the clients must pay their own way, but a legitimate learning opportunity in a nice location is a perfectly ethical and legitimate option to offer.
- Create an "advisory board" of past clients with whom you're sure you will not be doing additional business

directly (or you will run into ethical issues), and meet with them twice a year in person and twice a year by virtual means. Explain the status of your business—its offerings and current positioning—and ask for advice and direction. In return, you can offer board members your advice on their own careers and business challenges.

- Nominate past clients to positions you find that might be highly pleasing: board seats, media interviews, award nominations, keynote speaking opportunities, and so forth. There is no direct conflict of interest, since you haven't done business with their firm lately.

The idea with all of these techniques is to create an ongoing communications loop with all clients, past and present, so that you are constantly (or at least frequently) on their minds. This is a "timing" business, in that your name must appear in proximity to someone else's expressed need. No matter how appropriate the need, if no one thinks of you, you can't be referred. And no matter how visible you are at the moment, if there is no need, you can't be referred.

So, on the assumption that past buyers will periodically encounter needs that you can meet, it's vital that you maintain both aggressive and passive visibility, and remain involved with these buyers, no matter where they may go.

Keep in mind that retired executives are often named to major boards, to head prominent nonprofits, to teach at major universities, and to become guest columnists. Many pursue independent publishing and speaking careers. The leverage potential of your past clients is vast, and it is not confined to the job in which you originally partnered with them.

CHAPTER 9

THE DIAMOND STANDARD

CREATING RETAINERS AND EVERGREEN CLIENTS

CONVERTING TO "ACCESS TO YOUR SMARTS"

This entire chapter is on retainers. That's because these are in your "vault" on the Accelerant Curve (see page 26). Retainers provide the long-term relationships that excellent consultants deserve. Unfortunately, most consultants believe that their project's end *is also the relationship's end.*

The project and the buyer relationship are two entirely different dynamics. That's why you should establish a trusting relationship first. It can lead to many projects and to retainer relationships. You don't have to worry about the "active" and "inactive" clients of the previous chapter if you have perpetual clients.

And that's what retainers provide.

Attorneys collect a "retainer" that is really merely a deposit against their ongoing (ridiculous) hourly billing in six-minute increments. (If wealth is really discretionary time, imagine

> ### Listen Up!
> *A retainer is not a deposit. It is a fee paid for the value of access to your "smarts." An attorney's retainer is to a true retainer as McDonald's is to fine food.*

entering a profession in which, in order to make money, you have to track and maximize the use of every twelfth of an hour!)

For consultants, the retainer of which I speak is a price paid for access—not days of access, duration of access, or instant access, but merely access. There are three variables that determine retainer fees, and these do not exist in traditional projects (which are based on *objectives* to be met, *metrics* to evaluate progress, and the *value* to the organization of meeting those objectives).

1. *Who?* How many people have access to you during the course of the retainer? Is it solely your buyer, or is it also two of his reports or three of her colleagues? For pragmatic and responsiveness reasons, it's seldom more than four or so. But the more people who have access, the more valuable that access is, and the higher your fee.

2. *How?* Is access during business hours Eastern U.S. time, which is where you're located; Western U.S. time, which is where the client is located; or to accommodate London time, where a key subsidiary is located? Is access solely remote—e-mail, phone, Skype, virtual meeting, and so on? Or will you be expected to meet in person at designated, mutually convenient times? The wider and more flexible the access, the more valuable the access.

3. *When?* What is the duration? Generally, a month is far too little, with insufficient time to test, try, respond, and review issues. A quarter is a typical minimum, but a half-year or annual retainer is not uncommon. The longer the access, the more valuable it is. (It's often impossible for an organization to extend a retainer beyond the limits of its current fiscal year because of its own fiduciary procedures.)

When you've completed a project (or, better, several projects), it's an ideal time to convert to a retainer relationship, unlike most consultants, who pack their bags and move on. Sometimes the buyer will suggest something, such as, "I wish there were a way to keep you involved here, but I have no current projects that make sense."

CASE STUDY: The Calgon Emergency

The president of Calgon had me on retainer for five years. During the third year, which included personal visits, he called me one evening and told me that there was an emergency that required the entire field force to be assembled in Pittsburgh during the coming weekend. He needed me to facilitate the session so that it stayed on track and because I didn't represent any internal interest group.

I changed my schedule, my wife understood, and I spent the weekend in Pittsburgh.

In the fourth and fifth years of the retainer (before Calgon was sold), the president unilaterally raised my retainer fee by 30 percent, to $130,000. "You're more valuable than the fee you've set," he said, and for only the second time in my life, I was speechless.

These are the "vault" items that create perpetual clients and eternal referrals.

Sometimes, you'll be required to broach the issue, such as, "Gloria, I was thinking that the special relationship I have with some of my very best clients might now make sense for you." Some clients will be familiar with retainers, and some will not. In both cases, however, you'll have to educate the buyer about how yours works (see points 1 to 3 in the previous list).

This past year, in one of the meetings of the Million Dollar Consulting® Million Dollar Club, which I run, a very successful consultant from Australia had a fascinating insight: "I ought to stop looking at your business models compared to my own," he said, "and start realizing that I have access in these meetings to the minds that are advising top organizations all over the world. It's the advice, not the business model, that's valuable."

This same phenomenon holds true with your own clients. Their ability to access your "smarts" on a real-time, as-needed basis is invaluable. From your own observations with the client organization, you can come up with specific reasons, but here are some generic ones to consider:

- The buyer has conflicts among his or her own staff that need an objective resolution.
- There is a need for ongoing access to best practices, which you are constantly evolving from your work with dozens of clients.
- A major announcement or initiative needs to be rehearsed and/or improved before it goes "live."
- There is confidential information and plans that can't be trusted to internal people for discussion.
- There is an ethical issue that needs honest and disinterested analysis and debate.
- Surprises arise that take far too much time to deal with in the normal meetings or interactions, and would be facilitated by instant access to you.

Add your own reasons to my simple list. You only have to help with one or two essential decisions, problems, innovations, plans, conflicts, and so on before the retainer seems like the best bargain in the world and, as in my case study, the client is suggesting that you've been too low-priced!

Retainers create perpetual clients and eternal referrals. The client also realizes that providing a referral for you doesn't endanger your priority with that client at all, since this is a very low-labor-intensity relationship. (You can handle a great many retainers, but just multiply a dozen of them by $100,000 each, and then by two referrals per month.)

Ironically, the greatest difficulty with retainers is inside your own head.

GUILT-FREE RELATIONSHIPS WHEN PEOPLE RARELY NEED YOU

I receive frequent calls from consultants who ask what to do when they are on retainer and the client has barely utilized their help. Most want to "roll over" the days and extend the duration, sort of like a competitive offer from the cell phone people.

I tell them all to do absolutely nothing, because

- The client is an adult who knows when to call and how and is making intelligent choices. The client is not "damaged," and you are not the client's parent.
- The value you provide is in being available and accessible. A fire extinguisher or insurance policy is very valuable in case of fire, but you still hope you never have to use them except in a particular instance and exigency.

- The reason you're even asking is that you feel guilty and your low self-worth is bothering you. (A tad harsh, perhaps, but why else worry when a client is happy just knowing you're there, but you're not happy unless the client has some problem requiring your involvement?)

The value you bring to retainers (and, therefore, to evergreen clients) is in your acknowledged expertise, your accessibility, your rapid responsiveness, and your rapport and trust with the client. If retainers are the key to long-term referrals, then patience and confidence are the keys to retainers.

Listen Up!
Don't fall into the trap where the client who is placing you on retainer actually has more confidence in you than you do in yourself.

Think about this equation: over six months, the client calls you twice, once with a minor matter, and once with a major matter. The combination of your advice and counsel results in the client's saving a couple of days of time, making a decision with far more confidence, and avoiding a rash decision that would have required a $50,000 investment. The sum total of the tangibles is about $125,000; the intangibles provide lower stress and greater leadership mien; and the peripheral benefits are some important learning.

You're charging a $10,000 monthly retainer, meaning that at that point, you've been paid $60,000 (or slightly less if it was discounted for full payment in advance). Conservatively, that's about a 3:1 return right there.

You can't afford (literally, *afford*) to equalize time and money in this relationship. The amount of time you spend talking to the client is irrelevant. The quality of your advice and the safety and comfort of knowing that you're there are the valuable elements.

Marshall Goldsmith is the author of *What Got You Here Won't Get You There*. He's a world-renowned coach and a friend, and he was my guest at my first Thought Leadership Workshop. He and I agree completely on this phenomenon: the people whom we tend to help the most are those whom we tend to work with the least. Neither of us demands strict regimens and periodic contact.

One of the most successful people in the history of my Mentor Program—which is, in effect, a retainer, with participants having access to me over agreed-upon time frames—is currently making about $5 million as a solo practitioner. Every December, he sends in a full year's retainer for the ensuing 12 months. We usually talk no more than twice a quarter, for about 10 minutes each time. These conversations are always on critical decisions

---

CASE STUDY: **The High-Tech Tremors**

One of my retainer clients was the founder, with five colleagues, of a high-growth, high-tech firm. After several projects, I went on retainer. We didn't speak often, as the firm stabilized and grew according to its strategy.

However, the client called me twice one year. Once was to facilitate a meeting with some anxious investors who didn't feel they were seeing their return rapidly enough. Another was a phone conversation to work through the departure of two of the original partners, as painful as that was, because of a reassessment of need as the firm grew.

"For those two instances alone," my client confided, "you were worth the price of admission."

In Disneyland, once upon a time, they used to call that an "E-ticket," meaning that you could get on any ride in the park at any time.

and key pricing issues, where he solicits my ideas and anticipates client resistance, and we both work to overcome it.

Some clients *will* need you often. You will have to decide whether they are having legitimate, frequent need for a sounding board, or whether you are some kind of "crutch" to keep them from falling. You want to be a coach, not co-dependent. When clients do need you often, it's still usually a few times a month on the phone or by e-mail. Don't make short issues into lengthy ones, and don't allow easy challenges to become complex.

In working with a nonprofit that needed to increase unearned income, I heard a consultant say that his retainer work was currently to advise on a model to secure more donations from high-potential, wealthy individuals.

"Isn't that a matter of building relationships between the organization's key officers and those donors?" I asked.

"Yes," he admitted, "that is the model."

"Well, that's no model, that's common sense, and you can talk about how to go about that in 10 minutes. Don't make things complex. That doesn't make them more valuable; it merely makes them more labor-intensive."

What happens if the retainer client hasn't called? Shouldn't you do *something?!* Well, yes, because your primary personal goal is to stimulate referrals for the duration of the retainer, and on an ongoing basis. So here are some practices that make sense without throwing yourself under a bus:

- If you haven't heard from the client in a 30-day period, make a call (not an e-mail) and say that you're simply checking in, which is your practice when you haven't been in contact for about a month. Do *not* offer to do any work; just offer to listen.

- Think of the prior time the client called for help or advice, and send something additional, such as tips from other clients, with this note: "I was thinking about our last conversation and thought that this material might be of additional help."

• Offer the client an opportunity, such as to coauthor a newsletter or blog article, that will force a response and further communication.

Your most important trait in a retainer, aside from the value and responsiveness we've discussed, is to be calm and guilt-free. You can handle multiple retainers, and many of us have. But you can't do that if you're feeling guilty about each one that doesn't call you weekly or more often!

Bear in mind that your best clients are performing the best, have asked you for situational help in the past, and will ask you again in the future when they see the need. But by definition of being "the best," that really won't be all that often.

THE PICASSO RULE: YOU KNOW WHERE TO PUT THE PAINT

There is a story about Picasso's mother telling him that he was so talented that if he joined the clergy, he would become Pope, and if he joined the military, he would become a great general.

"But instead I took up art," he said, "and I became Picasso."

Picasso is also most commonly cited as the artist who admonished people who pointed out that he painted rapidly and that it took him only seconds to apply blue paint, "Ah, but it's taken me a lifetime to understand *where* to apply the blue paint."

Your relationship with these "evergreen" clients must be one of that level of expert status. You must welcome the opportunity to be seen as the expert who is rarely needed, but who is invaluable when accessed. That means that in addition to not

> ## Listen Up!
> *Your value is in the unique combination of your experience, expertise, and execution. It has nothing to do with time, frequency, or duration.*

feeling guilty about your client's infrequent contact while you're on retainer, you must also be willing and comfortable in grasping the expert's role with pride and not insecurity.

Bill Russell, the great Boston Celtics basketball center who led his team to multiple championships, said in his book *Second Wind* that it's not the everyday play that makes someone a standout, but rather the ability to perform at the top of one's game when under the greatest possible pressure. He was talking about playoff games that were tied in the fourth quarter. I'm talking about the legitimate inquiries from your retainer clients who are desperate for world-class advice.

These are the fourth quarters of your playoff games.

Figure 9.1 is an important aid for you.

CASE STUDY: That's Why We Hired You

The senior vice president of human resources at Merck (a rare HR guy who was superb at working with line officers and finding them the right resources) had asked me to outline briefly how a certain internal project should advance.

I gave him three options, which is what I do in proposals, but this was a case where I was dealing with a long-term retainer arrangement.

"Alan," he said, "we're not paying you to tell us we have options and to choose one. We're paying you to tell us which option is best for us."

I never forgot that lesson, and I never confused my marketing with my implementation again.

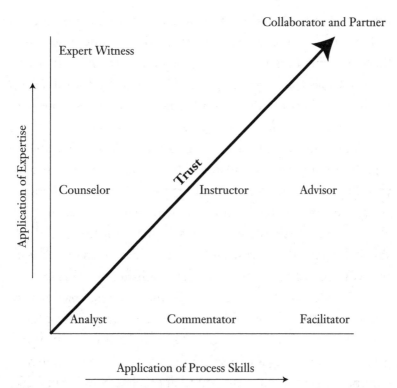

Figure 9.1 The Roles of a Consultant

The retainer role is that of a collaborator and a partner. You are applying your native process skills (strategy, conflict resolution, decision making, and so forth) in combination with your knowledge of that client (politics, content, personalities, and so on) so as to be of particular and highly focused help when accessed. (This is why retainer relationships almost always make the most sense *after* a series of projects, when you have acquired that organization's content knowledge.)

My diagonal line is the trust line, which is built on the synthesis of your best practices elsewhere and your best knowledge of that client. This is why my Merck contact in the case study correctly expected a specific recommendation—crisp and succinct—not a range of options requiring further debate and investigation. This is also why it's so difficult for other consultants to dislodge consultants who are entrenched in retainer business—those combinations are simply too powerful to replace. In effect, the client has spent far too much educating the consultant on retainer to sacrifice that resource just because someone else comes along who claims to be better or less expensive.

The impact on referrals is enormous. As you are able to rapidly provide the articulated expertise at the right time for your buyer, your credibility and repute will grow, and people's confidence in recommending you will also increase, since it's clear that very little of your time is required for these relationships. There isn't the constant fear that there is in client work that you won't have time or will have shifting priorities.

My Mentor Program, as I've mentioned, is a form of retainer, and I've handled more than 30 active people at once and currently have more than 1,000 people in the entire program in various stages of activity. (See my earlier comments on communities that will help you to appreciate how retainerlike relationships can be managed through other people and through common experiences, with the value accruing to you.)

"Knowing where to put the paint" and being able to do so under the pressure of a close championship game are the keys to your retainer success. And your retainer success is the key to lifelong referrals. *Your mindset must be that referrals are future revenue and current business is today's revenue, and that both are equally important for your business. That's the essence of this book, and that's why it isn't merely a postscript in my other books, such as* Million Dollar Consulting.

I've come to realize this relatively late in my career, so I hope this Picasso effect will help those of you who are veterans to become even better at referral business, and those of you who are newer to gain the right habits much earlier than I did, thus ensuring your own futures at an earlier stage in your own careers.

Referrals can come intermittently from people who merely know you (or who have simply heard of you); they can come periodically from those who have been clients, especially with aggressive pursuit on your part; but they can become perpetual with little or no prodding on your part when you create retainer relationships on a large scale. These are the apotheosis of both evergreen clients and perpetual referrals. And they are the least labor-intensive to acquire and to deliver in most cases.

We'll go on to examine how to price these retainers (since they represent current revenue, and you might as well maximize that, as well) and how to prompt their acceptance. Just bear in mind that you are creating immense benefit when you create these relatively rare relationships, and that you are cashing in on only half of the benefit if you don't consider future revenue as well—referral business.

PRICE GUIDELINES FOR RETAINERS

Price consideration for retainers is important because you'll be setting a precedent for your referral business. Since retainers are *not* based on projects with objectives, metrics, and value, they can be harder to price and to justify. Remember the three considerations for retainer fees: (1) Who: how many people have access? (2) How: to what extent do they have access? (3) When: what is the duration of the access?

Fee setting is always both art and science, but let's revisit the formula that represents the vital two dimensions, since we can create discipline in fees. First, Figure 9.2 shows the vital dimensions.

The more the buyer is committed and sees a high fee as justified in terms of return on investment, ego reward, and justification, the more you have a reciprocity (upper right quad-

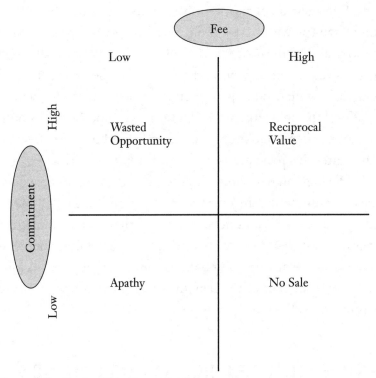

Figure 9.2 The Fee/Commitment Relationships

rant), meaning that the buyer finds you valuable and you find the buyer valuable. If the buyer is highly committed to your worth, but you don't charge sufficiently, you've wasted the opportunity. Obviously, if buyer commitment is missing (below the horizontal line), you'll have no sale or a poor sale. These aren't going to result in retainers.

So the buyer has to believe in the value of the access to your smarts, something that is most easily provided and established through the great return on prior engagements and projects, which is why retainers seldom are the first relationship you have with clients (unless you have a sterling brand and great intellectual property, such as highly regarded commercial books).

Then there is the "formula" that we can apply to retainers as well as to projects that provide direct and indirect benefits (see Figure 9.3).

In a retainer, the tangible outcomes would include immediate applicability of the advice, rapid change in the situation, problem quickly solved, decision immediately made, conflict rapidly resolved, and so forth.

The intangible outcomes might include stress relief, warring factions defused, increased confidence in decision making, precedents set, future decisions made at proper levels, and so on.

The peripheral benefits would be represented by greater confidence in the buyer's decisions, increased appreciation by the board, transfers of skills, knowledge that events will be quickly reconciled, and so forth.

As you consider these factors, we'll add to the "art" of the art and science. (1) Why you, why now, why in this manner? If a great many people could provide this expertise and responsiveness under similar circumstances, then you're less valuable. But if you are alone in that capacity, you're very valuable. And why now? Is there a window of opportunity or a period of threat that makes your counsel more critical than at any other time? And why in this manner? Has your buyer attempted this before with others or internally and found the process to be weak? Does your position and repute represent the "last best chance" (to quote Lincoln)? (2) Your buyer's ego is at stake. Buyers don't usually say, "I have the cheapest consultant on retainer I could find," or "I've decided to retain that guy who did so poorly on projects here so that he can screw up still more." Instead, they

$$\frac{\begin{array}{l} \text{Tangible Outcomes} \times \text{Expected Duration of Outcomes } + \\ \text{Intangible Outcomes} \times \text{Emotional Impact of Intangibles } - \\ \text{Peripheral Benefits } + \text{Variables Positively Affected} \end{array}}{\text{Fixed Investment Required}} = \text{Client's "Good Deal"}$$

Figure 9.3   The Fee Formula

say, "Joan is very expensive, but her work for us and other world-class companies has been so outstanding that I've decided we must retain her as we embark on these challenging times."

You get the drift. In addition to the tangible, intangible, and peripheral benefits, there is a question of your uniqueness and the buyer's ego. *All* of these factors provide weight for your actual retainer fee.

Having established all of that, and while encouraging you to be aggressive in your own unique situations, here are some criteria to help you out.

First, the retainer arrangement should be for a minimum of three months (a quarter of a year). There is insufficient time in shorter periods to allow for the ebb and flow of buyer needs, for trial and error, and for experimentation. Monthly retainers make no sense to me for that practical reason alone. If the buyer doesn't use your help in a month, the party is over.

Second, the limit on the number of people from the client who have access to you in a retainer relationship should be three. If you're truly accessible without limit, then you can't afford to have too many people from a single client. Moreover, you must ensure that all these people are of about the same level, such as the CEO and two direct reports, or three line vice presidents.

Third, payment terms should always be at the beginning of the period, with an incentive if needed. In other words, a 90-day retainer is due and payable at the outset of the 90 days, a half-year retainer at the outset of the half-year (perhaps with a 10 percent incentive for full payment), and so forth. Allowing for monthly payments is leaving the door wide open for a minion in accounting or procurement to point out that, since no contacts were made over the prior 30 days, no payment should really be due. These low-level people don't think in terms of the value of your being there, but rather in terms of boxes on grids being filled in.

Fourth, the retainer should never be for less than $5,000 per month as an absolute minimum, and that probably only for smaller businesses. Given the previous criteria, I suggest that your fees be at a minimum of $7,500 per month and up. Retainers of $25,000 per month are not uncommon at senior levels of Fortune 1000 organizations (former executives are often pulling in six figures per month on "retainer" arrangements).

Don't accept monthly payments and provide incentives for longer periods, so that a $10,000 monthly retainer becomes only $100,000 for the year if it's paid in full on January 2. In the case of a true emergency—such as an executive's illness, a company disaster, or sudden resignations—I do allow retainers to be extended, but only if payments are made as originally agreed.

RETAINERS FOR LIFE (AKA "THE VAULT")

We've reached the extreme right of the Accelerant Curve, which I've reprinted in Figure 9.4. This is the "vault" area, which is beyond "breakthrough" and is your personal turf and domain, with unique value to your client.

How do you create what are, in effect, "retainers for life"? How do clients become permanent and perpetual, providing an endless stream of referrals and endorsements?

No single client will probably ever be permanent. I'm sure you can cite an exception or two, but even Peter Drucker didn't work with General Motors continually (although he might have literally invented strategy as we know it while working with Alfred P. Sloan there).

The key (combination?) to the vault is to have a large number of retainer clients so that they are replenishing themselves or being replaced by newer ones. Retainer clients can

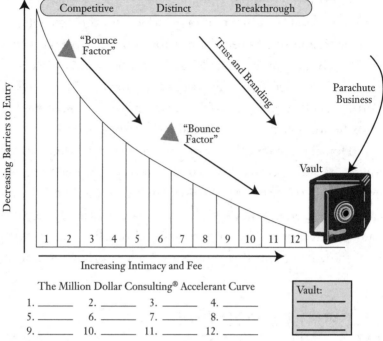

The Million Dollar Consulting® Accelerant Curve

1. _____   2. _____   3. _____   4. _____
5. _____   6. _____   7. _____   8. _____
9. _____   10. _____   11. _____   12. _____

Vault:
_____
_____
_____

Figure 9.4   The Accelerant Curve and the Vault

- Be with you for many years.

- Leave and come back.

- Drop out permanently.

- Be replaced by newer retainer clients.

When you hear a choir sing an especially long note, it's because some members are sustaining it while others take a breath, then others sustain it while the first group takes a breath. What the audience hears is a single, lengthy note that was continued through collaboration.

What you can achieve are "permanent" retainer relationships created by an overlap of those coming, going, and returning. It's vital that you maintain a sufficient number of retainer clients to "hold the note."

> **Listen Up!**
> *View your client list as a cumulative one, where you want to maintain a certain critical mass of concurrent business, not merely sequential business.*

In looking at Figure 9.4, you can appreciate that as you take clients through projects down the Accelerant Curve, it is easier to create retainer relationships. However, as your brand and your thought leadership grow, you will also derive the "parachute business" on the right, which might immediately begin as retainer business.

I'm suggesting that this "diamond standard" of evergreen clients needs to be nurtured, fed, and pruned, so that while there may be turnover, there will always be a critical mass pres-

CASE STUDY: We Need Smart People Here

I was introduced by a subordinate (I was referred to the subordinate by an existing client, and she paved the way for me to meet her boss) to a senior vice president at Marine Midland Bank (now a part of HSBC). Over the course of our allotted 45-minute meeting, I rather desperately tried to figure out a need that was being expressed that I could help meet.

The vice president was cordial and open. He apologized after 40 minutes, saying, "I'm sorry that time went by so quickly, but I must go to another meeting. Call me next week and we'll set up a relationship with you so that you can help us."

Happy but bewildered, I blurted out, "Help you with what?"

"Oh, I don't know," he said, "but I do know we need smart people around here, and you're smart, so we need to find a way to keep you around and have access to you." (I went on to work for this individual in three successive organizations he joined.)

ent. And that critical mass will be producing passive (un-solicited) referrals for you on a figurative round-the-clock basis.

If your doctor has 300 patients, 10 percent of them refer new patients to her, and 2 percent leave because of death or relocation, then the doctor has 324 patients at the end of that year. If the same proportions continue to hold true, then the next year the doctor has 350 patients. Doctors routinely receive passive referrals from happy patients, and many of the finest general practitioners today (individual care physicians) don't take on new patients except by referral. They are renewing their referrals and their patient numbers without trying.

The same holds true for consultants.

You can sustain that long referral "note" by focusing on retainer business, which is the business that is most likely to provide you with passive referrals. "Out of sight, out of mind" is more than an observation—it's a threat. And absence does not make the heart grow fonder; it makes the brain forget.

Project-based work that expires and leads to disengagement can be effective in providing referrals during its life, but not as much after the projects end. Retainer business keeps you omnipresent, even if you're not actually contacted daily (or even weekly). The client knows you're there, and you can readily raise your profile at whatever point you like.

Most consultants have not looked at retainer business as a natural evolution from project business, nor have they considered the cumulative effect of concurrent retainer clients.

Now that you are on board with these concepts, let's turn to the disciplines you can apply to create round-the-clock referral business.

CHAPTER 10

THE KALEIDOSCOPE

THE DISCIPLINE
AND FOCUS FOR
PERMANENT
REFERRALS

REFERRALS FROM COLLEAGUES

I'm using the term *colleague* here in a nonclient, nonbusiness sense. I'm using the term to embrace people who don't have direct business relationships with you. We've discussed them in portions of other chapters, but I thought a few dedicated pages in our focus on "permanent referrals" made sense.

You're providing collegial referrals on an ongoing basis. Not long ago, the woman who runs the teleconferencing service I use and the man who runs the automated listservs for my multitude of newsletters both dropped me a line and thanked me for referring so many people to them. A man who runs a source for press interviews wrote to tell me that he was delighted to be mentioned in one of my books.

All of these calls surprised (and pleased) me, because they were unexpected and also indicative of the undoubted reciprocity that was going on. I realized that I should be thanking people more often, as well.

Who are these people? Well, they can surprise you. Here are some examples that pertain to consultants and other professional services providers that may surprise you in terms of their effectiveness and omnipresence:

- Reviewers of your books on Amazon.com and similar venues. Find out how to contact them (Google, LinkedIn, and so forth) and provide a brief "thanks" for their courtesy.

- Blog mentions. I use vehicles such as Google Alerts (which is free) to learn daily where my name and trademarks are being used. So if Alan Weiss or Million Dollar Consulting was used on the Internet the day before, I can investigate. (By-product: I can also see when someone else has "appropriated" my work, and I can also find out what the competition is up to.) There is almost always the opportunity to leave your own comment, and I thank people for their favorable mention of my work. This encourages further mention in most cases.

- Mentions in newspaper articles. When you're mentioned in a newspaper article (online or hard copy), you're tacitly being referred by highly credible third parties (both the reporter and the publication). Make it a practice to compliment the reporter when the piece is published, keep the reporter on your contact list, and suggest new ideas for similar articles with your participation. I've been contacted by reporters years after the original interview because reporters maintain meticulous lists of contacts and sources.

- People who endorse you during appearances. When you're making a speech or delivering a workshop, there are often people singing your praises who have been in your groups before, read your work, or otherwise availed themselves of your value. It's a good idea to "seed" your events with these "live" referral sources by offering them complimentary admission.

Listen Up!
Referrals are occurring continually, as you are reading this. You want to do everything possible to be in this torrent.

- People who provide services for you in general. The key is to ensure that this myriad of support people is sufficiently knowledgeable about what you do to be able to refer you to others effectively. You can accomplish this by giving away free books, articles, Web site locations, and so forth. I've never considered my books as huge sales generators (although I got lucky with a few of them). Rather, I see them as highly effective marketing devices that I give out with the same flourish that others use with business cards. Which people does it make sense to educate? More than you'd think:

Yard workers	Repairpeople	Postal delivery person
Printers	Designers	Maintenance people
Painters	Couriers	Dog walkers

What do these people have in common? If they're supporting you, they're supporting others like you, and they have a vested, competitive interest in helping all of their clients in any way they can.

You may conclude that these types of referrals are strictly within the community and the local business potential. However, you probably don't work solely in the immediate community; in fact, you probably work outside of it most of the time. Similarly, these other individuals will often have interests and contacts outside of the immediate community. They may be part of larger businesses, or commute to another city, or have colleagues all over the world.

Moreover, the kind of support people I'm referring to here generally work within narrow economic strata. If you have achieved a certain level of success, then their clients are generally your peers, so they are working for other executives and professionals.

We'll talk a bit later about stimulating these dynamics by providing referrals of your own.

But before we conclude this topic, I'll suggest some action plans for you.

1. List those individual service providers who most probably also work for potential clients and recommenders and talk to them casually about your work, just as they'll be happy to talk to you about theirs. (If they've already benefited from referrals that you provided, then ask them how those referrals have worked out.)

2. Provide them with some effective material in a brief form that they can use if someone else asks about you. For example, if someone says that he has a client who has often mentioned that he needs help in one of my areas of expertise, I'll give that person two books—one for herself, and one to pass on to her other customer. You can't expect this person to market you, but your materials can help market you.

3. List those service owners who probably also work with potential clients and recommenders. Leave your book or materials in their businesses if there is a space to do so. (Recently, in my huge suite at the Ritz-Carlton in Berlin, I noticed a large wall of books. I had more than I needed for the program I was delivering, so I placed two of mine neatly on the shelves!) Many of these businesses compare notes in chambers of commerce, Rotary meetings, service clubs, and so on.

4. Focus on events where key people assemble—such as special events nights at social clubs or trustees' meetings of a nonprofit—and provide your value at every opportunity. It will be seen as your contribution to the cause, but it will inevitably serve as a showcase for your talents to those who may refer you to others.

Some of the best referrals I've ever had surprised me, because I had not been doing anything aggressive, but was merely keeping active in a variety of areas, and understanding that anyone around me who expressed interest in my work was worth talking to and giving something to.

WEEKLY ROUTINES

Well, what about the nitty-gritty, granular trench work that needs to be done on a regular basis? When you start to implement the practices we've been discussing, you have to put a plan of action in process.

I often ask people whom I mentor to keep a log of their time use over two weeks, and compare it with what they *thought* was occupying their time. They usually think that marketing and delivery are predominant, but what they find are huge "time dumps" dedicated to administration, e-mail, social media platforms, and general distraction.

So if referrals represent future revenue, then they must take a priority in your *planned* priorities. Here are my recommendations, with flexibility for your own particular practice, disposition, and prospect list, for things to do on a weekly basis, in no special order:

1. See the Man

The police have traditionally broadcast "see the man" at certain addresses to direct their patrol cars. You need to physically (not virtually) meet with people who can help you. Therefore, each week, you should be scheduling

- Networking opportunities
- Meetings with current clients during which you ask for referrals
- Meetings with past clients to seek referrals
- Interactions with social and civic colleagues at clubs, events, charitable affairs, and so forth

2. Raise Your Voice

Seek out opportunities to be interviewed in the media. This includes broadcast, hard-copy print, and electronic. You may not appear every week, but I'm suggesting that you pursue this every week. If you simply wait for it to happen, well, what happens when you merely wait for the phone to ring? It gets quite lonely.

- Suggest interviews to talk show producers.

- Join and respond to reporter inquiry services (for example, PRLeads.com or ExpertClick.com).
- Find very popular bloggers who might benefit from an interview with you (be discriminating here; tiny audiences of unknowns won't help you).
- Find panel opportunities where you can spread your value and be perceived as a peer of respected colleagues on the panel.

3. Pound the Keys

Use your initiative to contact people (or invite contact with you) through hard and electronic copy that you initiate. Do not consider social media to be an effective aspect of this. You don't want your voice lost in the din of the masses. Make yourself a unique source of value.[1]

- A monthly newsletter that goes to both clients and prospects is de rigueur, including client guest articles (which are, in fact, referrals).
- Create a blog to which people come (and can utilize RSS feeds) that includes testimonials and referrals in the postings and in constant margins of the publication.
- Mail to your overall database (as we've discussed at length) frequently, explaining new value and inviting referrals.
- Create intellectual property in the form of published articles, booklets, manuals, books, and so forth.

[1] I have about 3,000 followers on Twitter, but I follow no one. While that irritates a great many of the Twitter fanatics who actually believe that there is some bizarre etiquette involved, it also makes me an object of interest because of the dynamic. So if you do use social media, use them differently.

4. Pay Your Dues

Use the phone and e-mail to thank people who have helped you. Today, my bookkeeper of 10 years (who accepted a full-time controller's position) was replaced by a new one who was recommended by my tax accountants. After we had agreed on working together, she said, "Who recommended me? I want to call and say thank you." Two acts stimulate referrals more than all others: providing referrals yourself for others (which we'll discuss in the next segment) and thanking people who have provided them.

- If the person isn't financially involved in the new referral business and is not a current or past client, think about a gift or a favor.
- If the source is an independent one that can duplicate the referral many times over, consider a finder's fee (discussed in an earlier chapter).
- Send a handwritten thank-you note, not an e-mail, whenever possible.
- Keep your referral sources up to date on your progress with the person you referred.

5. Hit the Pavement

A woman asked today on my online forum what she should do: a client had happily referred her to three peers and copied her on the letters, but it's been 10 days since the letters went out, and none of the recipients has contacted her. She, of course, should have contacted the referrals within a few days of the letters' going out!

- Pursue referrals professionally but diligently, using the correct language from templates earlier in the book ("Paul has never given me bad advice about who can benefit from . . .").

- Travel expenses are a cost of doing business, so give people who are clearly buyers options for how you can visit them.

- Go to professional and trade association meetings where you're likely to meet people who are prospects mingling with people who have been your clients.

- Create breakfasts or luncheons where you deliberately "seed" clients into situations where prospects are present to learn and derive value.

Listen Up!
Even longer-term plans have to begin today.
Every week, you should be assigning time (setting
priorities) to the referral activities that will be most
efficacious for you in the short and long terms.

Time is not a resource. You have 24 hours in every day, but the *manner in which you spend it* is the key. Time is a priority issue. It's very important that you assign time to the areas mentioned previously (and others that you may find effective) to ensure that you are adequately pursuing referrals every week. Some efforts will take many weeks or even months to reach fruition—writing a book, for example. But if you don't begin it today, it's not going to happen tomorrow—or ever.

Build into your weekly calendar, Filofax, PDA, or whatever you use specific activities and times to accomplish these pursuits. Measure your effectiveness weekly by calculating the time you've actually spent. If you're successful in a frequent and focused pursuit of referrals through these disciplined sources, you'll find that you'll also generate referrals while you sleep, which I'll demonstrate at the conclusion of this chapter.

PROVIDING REFERRALS FOR RECIPROCITY

Another technique I've touched upon to stimulate referrals is to *provide* referrals. This creates an obligation and reciprocity with many people (although not all!). I noted earlier that both my teleconference and database providers were very appreciative of my spontaneous referrals to them.

Many people have commented that I've sent them more business than any other single source. I never accept referral fees, even if the situation would permit them. That's because *the referral in the future from that source is the value in which I'm investing—the ROI.*

Listen Up!
Of course you'll provide referrals regularly as a favor and a professional courtesy, without the expectation of reciprocity. But the more you do so and are deliberate about those referrals, the more reciprocity will emerge.

The more you stimulate key sources, the more you can expect favorable treatment in return. It takes some deliberate and disciplined approaches to create these dynamics, and they can be made part of the weekly routine we discussed earlier. Here are four essential steps in providing referrals that are perceived as high quality by those who can provide high-quality referrals in return.

1. Identify Your Targets of Opportunity

Start backward. That is, who are the people who are in a position to provide you with the highest-quality referrals? Are they current clients, past clients, community leaders, nonprofit executives, search firm partners, or professional association colleagues? Who are the people you want to target?

You can see immediately that while you may be freely providing referrals to your doctor or your accountant or your designer every day, these may not be the highest-priority reciprocity targets for you, so *in addition* to those courtesy referrals, you need to deliberately build in more.

2. Whom Would They Most Like to Meet?

Who are those people's buyers? You must provide quality in order to stimulate quality. Are they trying to meet wholesale buyers (for example, corporate executives), retail buyers (for example, individual consumers), or specialized individuals (for example, newspaper editors)?

This step is the pivotal point for what follows. Once you know your target, what people would constitute the *ideal* buyers for that target to meet? The last thing you want to do is to waste the target's time with nonbuyers or inappropriate ones. Put yourself in his shoes. For example, an auto dealer doesn't want someone who is merely looking for a car (ideally), but wants someone with an excellent credit rating who is looking for a top-of-the-line (highest-margin) model. The managing partner of a large accounting firm doesn't want to meet a finance director in a small business, but rather wants to meet the chief financial officer of a Fortune 1000 company.

3. How Will You Round Up the Usual Suspects?

Now you search your databases and lists and find the most likely suspects. This is a far higher-quality exercise than merely finding names. (Remember the earlier story about a woman who felt she had a great lead for me because she had read a story in a magazine about a European company that needed help?) This is a quality, not a quantity, exercise. A couple of high-potential names are always better than a slew of hit-or-miss lists.

You should be looking at

Your client list	Your subscription lists
Your vendors	Professional association colleagues
Social friends	Club and activity colleagues
Network acquaintances	Frequent e-mail contacts

Choose people who fit these criteria:

- Are clearly buyers for the target you have in mind.
- Have a need currently or one that can be developed commensurate with the target's offerings.
- See you as a credible and impartial source.

Now you have high-potential buyers for your targets. Obviously, the more targets you have and the larger your own network, the easier this becomes.

4. How Do You Maximize Your Contribution?

At this point, you want to make the most obvious connection you can. You don't want to merely give either party the other party's name and say, "I think this would be helpful." You want to obviously establish the connection. (Note that it's not impossible for *both* the referral and the target to be people who can reciprocate in the future, a sort of referral double whammy.)

Try to make the introduction in person. This can take place at a conference, an event, a community activity, a business trip, a social affair, or somewhere similar. It's always better to put people together in person if at all practical.

If distance or logistics preclude a personal introduction, then call your target and make the introduction by phone, establishing a good time for both people to talk and securing both their schedules and their preferences. This takes a bit of legwork, but it's well worth it because it adds immeasurably to your perceived value in the transaction. Too many casual introductions wind up with people playing phone tag and eventually attenuate. Set up a phone call and confirm with both.

Try to avoid e-mail introductions. They're easy, but that's the problem. By simply introducing Betsy to Jason with a "cc" (isn't it quaint that we still use "carbon copy" and "blind carbon copy"?), you've cheapened the quality of the introduction to something you simply did casually when you had time. There is no deliberate attempt here to forge a quality relationship.

Be personal at best; use the phone at worst. And then follow up. Find out if a meeting has been scheduled, what the result was, and so on. You can do this under the auspices of trying to provide better and better referrals for your target in the future.

I'm not being mercenary in suggesting that *in addition to* the referrals you provide out of courtesy and caring, you should *also* be proactively working on referrals that will result in dramatic reciprocity.

Andrew Sobell, a member of my Mentor Program, had met Marshall Goldsmith, the renowned coach and author. He introduced him to Chad Barr, who handles all of my technical work and is also in my Mentor Program.

Chad introduced Marshall to me. I invited him to appear at my Thought Leadership Workshop, which he did, and then provided a testimonial for my book *Million Dollar Coaching*. He is entertaining a proposal from Chad to completely reconfigure his Web presence.

Marshall invited Andrew to an awards ceremony, during which he introduced him to the president of Ford and the vice president of Wal-Mart. Andrew, Chad, and I recommend Marshall to anyone who will listen to us.

And so it goes.

THE REFERRAL REFERRAL (NO KIDDING)

I'm going to return to Hal Mapes, my case study in Chapter 1, to remind you of the exponential effect of referrals. Once a referral becomes a client, that person becomes a source for new referrals. Thus, if Hal had 200 insurance clients who gave him 6 names a year (1,200 referrals), and he closed 10 percent of them for new business (120), then the following year he had 320 clients and 1,920 referrals.

Once you start to extend this to the fourth and fifth years, you actually have a legal pyramid scheme, in that everyone "wins" and there are numbers to support the proposition. This is why I've been harping on the premise that referrals are future revenue, and therefore just as important as present revenue.

Let's see how this would work for you. You can record your answers right here in the book (if you don't like to mess up a book, then please buy another one to keep pristine!).

1. Record your current number of likely referral sources:

   Clients: ___

   Colleagues: ___

   Friends and family: ___

   Professional associations: ___

   Civic and social clubs: ___

   Vendors, suppliers, professionals: ___

   Other: ___

   Referral Sources, Total: ____

2. If you were to ask each person in this list twice a year for three names, estimate the percentage that would respond and multiply your total by that percentage:

   ___percent times Total ___ above equals
   Net Total: ___

3. Of the net total, take 50 percent as those referrals who are legitimate buyers and who agree to talk to you:

   50 percent of Net Total ___ equals **High-Potential Total: ___.**

4. Of the high-potential total, apply what you feel your reasonable or historical or improving business close rate would be. (I would suggest that this number will be between 40 percent and 80 percent for most of you):

   My close rate ___ percent times the high-potential total ___ equals **Closed New Business Total: ___**

5. Multiply your closed new business total by your average sales revenue:

Closed new business total ____ times average revenue per sale $____ equals **New Referral Revenue Estimate:** ____

6. Now take your closed business total ____ and add it to your original total number of referral sources ____ for **Next Year's Total Referral Sources:** ____

Listen Up!

If you look at the process as exponential growth and not arithmetic growth, you will realize that you have more referral opportunities than you imagine. You have to use referrals to generate still more referrals.

Let's say that you have 100 current contacts, and that half of them give you six names, meaning that you'll have 300 potential referrals. Taking half of them, being conservative, means that you have 150 high-potential referrals. If your close rate is 40 percent (near the bottom of my scale), then you'll create 60 new clients (if your close rate were a dismal 10 percent, you'd still have 15 new clients). This means two things:

1. Your new revenue potential, if your average new business contract is $20,000, will equal $1,200,000.

2. Your next year's basic referral sources will equal 160.

Now, *cut all this in half.* You'll still have $600,000 in new business and 115 new referral sources.

I know what you're thinking: this is crazy. He's exaggerating. But that's why I held these equations until the end of the book. I didn't want to scare you away with your potential good fortune. *And none of this counts spontaneous referrals not instigated by you!*

This is the power of referrals. This is why the book is called Million Dollar Referrals.

Let's examine the variables to demonstrate how conservative I've been and how much you can actually control these numbers:

- First, you must be diligent and thorough in developing your current contact list. That means your doctor, your attorneys, prospects who did not become clients, family members, Little League committee members—everyone you can think of. Remember, your mindset has to be that you have tremendous value to bring to people, not that you're "bothering them" or "trying to make a sale."

- Second, you have to ask. If you don't ask, you don't get. And you have to ask not only for names, but for high-quality names, people who represent your true potential buyers, not just someone in the bowels of the organization. You have to position this as a win/win/win to encourage the other party to participate. You must practice the techniques I've created to stimulate this, such as providing referrals in order to create reciprocity.

- Third, you have to diligently, professionally, and relentlessly pursue the referrals. You can't play phone tag or send off a lonely e-mail. You must make contact to try to validate that the other party is a buyer, and if so, establish a personal meeting. Again, the mindset has to be that you have great value that you'd be remiss not to offer.

- Fourth, you have to have the closing skills to create a business relationship. Consider what the numbers given here would be if your closing rate with buyers were 80 percent and not 40 percent![2]

- Fifth, you have to institutionalize the process, so that it's ongoing and second nature. By the fourth and fifth years, you will be dealing with a seven-figure business and beyond.

The variables you control here include the numbers of contacts, closing rate, average number of referrals, average size of your sale, repeat business, and so on. In other words, I'm being highly conservative regarding how much future business rests in your referral system because repeat business from new clients isn't factored in, nor are spontaneous referrals that develop unasked and unsought.

I hope you can appreciate what happens when you put to work the skills and mental attitude that I'm suggesting throughout this book. Your business will never be the same, and your ability to grow becomes progressively easier and less labor-intensive. You'll be able to choose your clients and your lifestyle.

That's not a bad return for asking for three names.

REFERRALS WHILE YOU SLEEP

The route to a seven-figure practice is the one that leads to you. You can't develop that kind of business by knocking on doors or by networking. You must draw people to you. Once you do that, you have access to a global community of potential buyers across oceans, time zones, and cultures.

The goal of this book has been to help you create a "referral culture" around your practice so that you can easily elicit

[2] For the reader seeking help, I immodestly recommend my book *How to Acquire Business* (Wiley 2002).

referrals and spontaneously be the beneficiary of them, leading to a dynamically growing firm. This is a possible dream. Every day, your contemporaries are recommending movies, restaurants, doctors, attorneys, car dealerships, masons, chimney sweeps, and snow removal services for three simple reasons:

1. They believe in and have used the product or service personally, with salubrious results.
2. They have friends, associates, and colleagues with similar interests and needs in their own lives.
3. They want to be of help primarily to their colleagues, but often also to the person they are citing.[3]

Thus, there is a client evangelism that arises, only very indirectly for personal gain. It is one of the purest forms of Samaritanism you'll encounter: the honest intent to put together others who will mutually benefit.

This means that all parties must be in "good standing." In other words, if my accountants do good work, but they are sometimes rude or late, I may not refer others to them, figuring that I can put up with the discomfort, but that others may well be put off. Similarly, if my accountants are great, but if I find the person who is asking me about accounting help to be a blowhard who is constantly taking over conversations, why would I want to help him out? Finally, if I'm a lousy client of the accounting firm (I pay my bills late or constantly complain about the charges), or if I'm perceived as the blowhard, then neither of the other parties is going to solicit my referrals or accept them.

So what we have here is the three-way good deal shown in Figure 10.1.

---

[3] While it may be more personal with your doctor, you also are hoping that Apple or Singapore Airlines does more business because you are a customer and a fan.

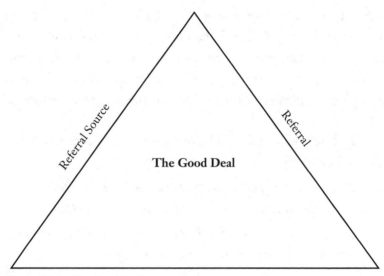

Figure 10.1   The Good Deal

This dynamic must persist and be self-perpetuating if you are to gain "referrals while you sleep." Your referral sources must believe in you, have had great experiences with you, have you in mind, and believe that you can help the third party's condition.

The referral must believe in the source's credibility, see you as a viable alternative, gain access to you readily, and like you.

Here are 10 steps to think about implementing or improving as soon as you end this chapter to maximize your opportunities with referral sources:

1. Keep your name and value in front of them on a regular basis.

2. Thank them promptly every time they refer someone.

3. Keep them apprised of additional value and offerings that you develop.

4. Ensure that they realize who the best referrals for you are.

5. Respond promptly to any request that they make.

6. Give them continuing value, personally.

7. Keep track of them so as not to lose contact with them if they move.

8. Maintain a high public profile in terms of media and publicity.

9. Invite them to events even if it is improbable that they can attend.

10. Provide them with referrals whenever possible.

And here are 10 steps to maximize the chances that a referral will do business with you:

1. Be accessible by phone, e-mail, regular mail, Skype, and so on.

2. Maintain a website with high credibility (not sales emphasis).

3. Ascertain that the referral is a buyer, then volunteer to visit.

4. Cite the referral source and the nature of that relationship.

5. Don't focus on what the referral wants, but rather on what he needs.

6. Focus on the referral's results, not your methodology.

7. Be highly responsive, demonstrating your service standards.

8. Provide value in the initial discussion.

9. Keep the referral apprised of offerings beyond what was cited.

10. Find low barriers to association (the left side of the Accelerant Curve).

Remember that all referrals can become superb referral sources themselves, since that's the manner in which they came to you.

Most of all, I want to leave you with one of our continuing refrains in this book: you must consider both current revenue and future revenue. The immediate business or project is your current revenue, but the referrals that emanate from that current business are your future revenue. You must jettison the mindset that referrals are some sort of "extra" or attractive aspect that you'd like to get around to. That's like saying you'd like to "get around to" a proposal for current business.

You require a proposal to close current business. You require referrals to close future business.

Referrals of the scope and nature that we've discussed comprise both art and science. The science is in the discipline, questioning, and follow-up. The art is in knowing when the time is right, the mood is appropriate, and the conditions are correct. I'm telling you that the art is ready for you far earlier than you might have otherwise believed.

So right here and now, you have a doubly powerful marketing approach, acquiring current and future business together. I hope I've helped a bit in that pursuit.

But think about something: how was it you came to know about me?

Listen Up!

Have you gained your 1 percent from this book? Can you do something better now than you formerly could? Can you garner more and better referrals? If so, do me a favor: refer someone to me! Thank you!

INDEX